EVA & DUANE ARE HERE TO SHARE THEIR REALEXPERIENCES FOR EVERYONE AS A

WORLDWIDE WAKEUP CALL!

ALLIS THE NATURAL ENVIRONMENT

Rebazar Tarzs

Duane The Great Writer

Ask Eva Now / Eva Knows

FEARING

IS KEEPING YU FROM YOUR REALADVENTURE

REPORTING THE REALNEWS

YU CAN 'ASK EVA NOW' ON FACEBOOK AND REBAZAR TARZS IN YOUR DREAMVISIONS

Duane

The Great Writer

2014

FEARING FEAR

"A Little Blue Birdy told me... "There IS Something NU under the Sun!" But, because it was a Little Blue Birdy, I was afraid! I always thought I was fearless, but I suddenly realized I was afraid of Something NU! I looked at myself very closely and wondered why I was so afraid of Something NU! Then I realized I have been taught to 'Be Afraid' of what I do not know or understand. This was a huge eye opener for me, and so I decided to Take The Risk and find out!" **Mr. Somebody**

Creation is something we are all in at this time. And while Being in Creation we have so many different things to deal with, and one of them is Fear. Fear is actually in everything we do, because we have made it so. Along with the Fear we have decided in our life, those who have Kreated the Kontrolling Systems use Fear against those who do not understand Fear to Kontrol others. Sometimes Fear is very obvious and we can deal with it, and then there is the fear that is cleverly hidden to 'Look' like something 'Good' when really it is not. It is true that most people do not want to 'Look' at the Fear they have or even discuss the Fear that exists in the world. But unknown to most people, until a person can See the Fear they have hidden within them, then are held by that Fear, and even for lifetimes of not knowing it exists with them at all. This is all a 'Choice' by each person to See the Fear they have, or they can pretend it does not exist. This is very understandable, because the physical life is hard enough to survive in.

There is a much bigger picture to Fear than the average person knows, and those in Kontrol of the earth know a great deal more than what the public does, because most people like their LA LA Land Life here. Fear is merely something we 'Agree' to. We each create our own Fears from the experiences we have. Fear is a matter of where our 'Attention' is. For myself, I have found one of the best ways to understand my Fears is to confront them and See them for what they are. Some people need others to help them, and some people would rather not deal with knowing what they carry with them all the time. I am constantly confronting what confronts me, as this is My Adventure and to make Better Choices for Myself, than to let the Fear that exists in this life Kontrol me. I have enough to deal with just knowing the OneWorld Order that Rules and Kontrols the earth also uses Fear as the main ingredient for all their Takeovers. Fortunately, the earth is just a 'Place in Life' and not Life ITSelf. I am fortunate to know there is So Much More than just being a physical person on this little earth.

The TruReality LifeIS, is all about Becoming MoreAware. But as we come into this life we are taught everything, but The TruReality LifeIS. So, each one of us must decide, or not decide, to discover what we have come to know as 'The True Meaning to Life,' which cannot be found with any Invented Institution such as the Political and Religious Systems would have YU 'Believe' in. From My RealExperiences with this life, I have come to 'Recognize' what most people have no idea can even exist at all, yet IT definitely does, but only with those who can first Recognize IT, and then PerSeeve The RealAdventure IT IS.

Creation has One Purpose Only, and that is for each of us to gain experience in this 'Simulation of Life' until we are each ready, one at a a time, to Take The Risk and explore what others will not. With all the varied experiences we have gained over thousands upon thousands of lifetimes, and at some point 'Recognize' The RealFreedom we have always sought. We must learn to Recognize what we have come thru, and then be introduced to The SoundLight Reality LifeIS, along with The RealGuidance and a RealEducation from The Real UNUversal Guides of THE ALLIS. With the TruRecognition of Creation, not the 'Invented Ideas' that people have been Educationally Dumbed Down with, but with What IS True & Real Now, YU, The RealU, are ready to take on 'A Journey to RealFreedom' when YU can Recognize the Comparison between 'What IS Real' and what is not, and then apply this to Your RealAwareniss to Recognize The TruReality, THE ALLIS. Here is where very few ever See Beyond Creation and the Gods of Man that have plagued mankind for eons. We each have Free Will, and in a way this is a burden or a blessing, but more than that, YU can Now have The RealFreedom YU have always wanted! Simply take the time to Read The NUBooks that make More Sense than anything!

EMOTIONAL ASSTRAL BODY TAPLINING

YU have a Physical body, YU have an Astral Body, YU have a Causal Body, YU have a Mental Body and an Etheric Body. It is The RealU, The RealAwareniss that occupies these Five Bodies for YU to Wake Up and Become MoreAware. This process takes millions of lifetimes in so many different types of embodiments. Most people are not aware there is so much more to themselves than what they see in the mirror. For those who want to discover who they really are, then this NUBook and the many others I have written will be of interest to YU. From our past lives and in our daily lives we are experiencing so many different aspects of this life. There is one particular reality that very few people are aware of, and this is TapLining in the Astral Body, and also the other bodies that effects the physical body. Many people are experiencing back pain, headaches, illnesses, diseases, cancers and even death from ASStral TapLining. The Medical Doctors can't detect TapLining, because it is in the other bodies, mainly the Astral Body, because this is the seat of the emotions for many people. I suggest a RealStudy of this for YU, because YU are being held against Your Will to situations YU are not aware of, unless YU do not mind the Effects of others Kontrolling Your Life. TapLining is centuries old and Real!

The Political, Religious, Spiritual, Educational, Social and Scientific Systems & Communities use TapLining to herd and Kontrol people to be subservient and to support their Natzee ideas. Not all the people of these systems do this, but in today's world, TapLining is a common practice that most people have no idea exists, because it works very well with keeping people unaware of their own TruNature and their RealAwareniss. The masses have been taught by the Religious and Political Korporations they 'have a soul' and that this 'soul idea' is a mystery. The Spiritual Systems are also telling people they are soul, as they have went a step further, but many times they are referring to the Astral Body of the person, as many spiritual groups do Astral Projection and 'Think' the Emotional Body of a person is their soul. The Astral Body is held to the Physical Body by what is known as the 'Silver Cord' and it must stay in tact for the physical body to survive.

TapLining happens in the back of the person where they do not See what is taking place. This is usually done in a Person's Dreams at night while they are unaware of this Kontrolling intrusion. When a person has an emotional 'Agreement' to something they will usually have a TapLine in them and sometimes a lot of them, and especially if the people who head the Korporation have a Kontrolling Intent which is many times unseen, because they 'hide' their true intent to the viewing audience, even though what they are doing 'looks good' many times it is not. I was taught by Paul Twitchell and his Corporation, who received The Rod of Power from Rebazar Tarzs. I personally know Darwin Gross and HarOld Klemp and his Reptilian Mate Joanny. Paul IS The RealGuide, as IS Rebazar & The Boys. Darwin and especially HarOld and his Seductive Wife are heavily TapLined, and they also TapLine their MemberShrimps where they are little captive animals on The RealSide. Old Master HarOld and Joanny secretly belong to the OneWorld Order in the Lower ASStral Realm, as this is their chosen life with what they are doing to others. They are a 'Rock-Solid' Korporation in the physical sense and not at all interested in The TruReality LifeIS, because then they would lose Kontrol, and Joanny would not be getting all the Power and Money SHE steals from HER unaware MemberShrimps. SHE is a very typical Earthly Korporation.

Also, the ideas of any type of 'Freedom' on earth from the Kontrolling Earthly Korporations(KEK) are altogether 'False!' There can never be any RealFreedom here, only 'implied freedom,' which is just an 'idea' of Marketing Ploy and nothing more. This is to keep people Dumbed Down and always 'Chasing' something that does not exist, but only 'seems' to exist in their Emotionally Stimulated Minds. The 'Love' idea is the same, as it is ASStral Emotional Stimulation with 'Pretty Words' and cute ideas attached, which make an excellent combination for the Reptilians to TapLine people in their dreams. RealLUV & RealSurvival are THE ALLIS, as IS RealTruth & RealFreedom, and RealGuidance IS Necessary to 'Recognize' this. We provide The RealEducation YU are looking for, moreso than the 'Old Love God' ideas of 'Worshiping and Praying' to Space Gods and 'Agreeing' to be TapLined with the Invented Restrictions that bind YU unconsciously into more lifetimes!!

REBAZAR TARZS IS THE REAL ADVENTURIST

Human History, as we have read about and come to know it with the Kontrolling Militarized Educational Systems, is not even close to what has taken place from what the hired historians have written and said. They have been paid to paint a picture according to what they have been told to write. Not all history is 'Slanted' but a lot of it is, and so much of what is reported on the news is purposely made to look like what it is not. Rebazar Tarzs is not found in any of the known history books, because those who want to have a Komplete Kontrol over others do not want them to know about Rebazar & The RealGuides.

RealFreedom and RealTruth cannot be found on the earth or with Creation, as so many have been led like sheep and cattle to 'Believe.' Everyone has their own 'Truth' and rightly so, because all of us have Free Will, and it is our right to make any choice we want, even if we are forced to make a choice. But, just because a person can have, decide, and choose anything they want does not mean they have the freedom they want, and especially RealFreedom. Rebazar is one of a very few who has always advocated RealFreedom, and for this he has been left out of Human History as The Wonderful Adventurist HE IS.

Rebazar Tarzs & The Real UNUversal Guides have taken on many 'roles' to 'Live The RealAdventure LifeIS!' This IS Real, but not really understood. Most people have been indoctrinated to 'Believe' that things like 'spiritualism, gods, masters, saviors and saints' and other such ancient references have something to do with The Whole of Life. The 'idea' of God Consciousness has been a long time favorite among many Spiritual Seekers for eons, but that was 'then' and This IS Now! LifeIS NUNow, and what was then is passed. Rebazar Tarzs & The RealGuides are so much more than what they have been 'labeled' as. They are no longer playing any roles like 'masters and gurus' are still doing who have not Become MoreAware of What IS Real Now. This is a Kontrolled World of Slave Drivers who whip the workforces day and night, and those who worship and pray to the Gods of Restriction are making their choice to stay TapLined to the Lower ASStral Worlds.

THE REALHISTORY OF THE REALGUIDES

Long before Jesus came to the earth and appeared before his time, The Real UNUversal Guides were planning what IS Now taking place with THE NUWAVIS THE NUMAN. Jesus was being trained by The RealGuides, but he decided to go out and take on his own adventure. It was his choice and The RealGuides watched him go. Jesus was one of many who was a student and at a certain time decided to test the waters of this world. What the masses have come to know is a tale told from the Kontrolling Systems, and it has nothing to do with The TruReality LifeIS, THE ALLIS. In time and space, long before Paul Twitchell appeared in this lifetime, The RealGuides already knew the future that was to take place according to the events that had already been laid out Cosmically and what could be Seen from The Real UNUverses of THE ALLIS. There would be a certain number of individuals who would be given the opportunity to take on the task and adventure of presenting 'Something Wonderful' to those searching for RealTruth and RealFreedom. Those struggling on the earth would never know any freedom from the Kontrolling Systems, because for the most part, mankind cannot Recognize THE ALLIS, as they have been bred to be subordinate to the worshiping of their Invented Gods.

It is a long road to any heaven after being on the earth for eons. Most people will settle for 'second best' just to get a taste of something better than what is on the earth. So, the Astral Worlds, The First Heaven of Man, seem to be a great place to rest between lifetimes. As the unaware struggle to SeeMore than just their bodies grow old, The RealGuides were setting into motion Something So Wonderful with what the earth world had never seen before. The RealGuides like The RealAdventure and Challenge of doing what others will not do in Creation. From The Unknown Real UNUverses, it is easy to See how those in Creation continue to fool themselves as to where they are and what is really taking place on earth and all the other Round Worlds. Because of the Free Will of those in the Physical Realm, The RealGuides can only enter at certain times to present Something Real, otherwise they wait for the right time to do so. People must learn to develop themselves before they can be ready for THE ALLIS. Before there was anything known as time, The RealGuides walked the RoundWorlds to assist those who had the smallest sign of wanting to Become MoreAware. There are many, many steps a person has to take before they can have The TruNitiation of THE IS. When Krone married Stage Master Harry, SHE began to Kontrol everything. SHE did not want me to have any more of the Fake Korporation initiations, and so Rebazar was giving me The TruNitiations on The RealSide.

Thousands of earth years before Paul came with his presentation, The RealGuides were preparing the way for THE NUWAVIS THE NUMAN. As anyone can see with Human History, there has been a lot of turmoil on the earth to get to this very moment. Many individuals were tested over the centuries, because it takes lifetimes of preparation for What IS Happening Now. As time and events progressed, many people were filtered out who could not See what had to be Seen with THE ALLIS. Slowly and patiently, The RealGuides were creatively and carefully moving everything into place that would be needed for The NUNowniss of THE ALLIS. As the time approached, which was still several lifetimes before The RealEvent, two of the Chosen Ones were having a bit of a struggle within their appointed lifetimes, and so The RealGuides stepped in to adjust some of the drama in their lives. At the same time, I was making it thru my lifetimes with Rebazar, as he was teaching me very directly. It soon came to my lifetime before this one where I was 'Goldie' (NUBook One / 'From Then To Now') The Golden Winged Warrior of THE ALLIS. Rebazar was training me very directly to get ready for The Modern Atomic Era of The Dumbed Down Humans. Before I took on a new body, Rebazar took me to THE ALLIS. I was shown who I would Now become during this life... 'DU THE NUMAN.' It was rather humorous as my earthly mother did not know what to name me at first, and so Rebazar showed her in a dream that she was to name me, Duane. At first she didn't remember her dream experiences, so she had the idea to look up a name in the telephone book, which Rebazar kept hinting her to do. Finally, as she went thru many names and did not like any of them, she saw the name Duane, and thought to herself, with the help of Rebazar, to give me the name Duane. And so it has come to be with The NUNowniss.

At the same time I was being prepared from lifetimes, Paul was also being readied, as he would set the pace to take 'The Rod of Power' first. From The Real UNUverses, I watched as Rebazar & The RealGuides escorted Paul into a new body. At first he did not care for the body Rebazar picked for him, because he saw that it was too short. Rebazar laughed and said, "Do you want to be a movie star, tall and handsome, so you will be distracted from what you will accomplish this lifetime?" Paul smiled and then went with Rebazar to the Body Station to prepare to enter the Physical Realm. As I watched Paul's birth and the family he went into, I knew I wanted to once again be next to the ocean. Rebazar knew this to, so the mother I was given would soon move to the Pacific Ocean in California. As Paul was being prepared at a very young age by Rebazar and his sister Katie, I was getting ready to enter my lifetime. I had been with Shiss on the Seventh Level and I really did not want to leave her, but I also knew The RealAdventure of The ALLAliveniss was calling me into action. I could See within My RealAwareniss there was a much Bigger Picture that would reveal itself as I took on The Real RiskTaker Position and task with the physical body on the Kali Kontrolled Earth.

So reluctantly, but wholeheartedly, I went with Rebazar and The Boys once more into the gloom of the PsycRealms and into the black space of where the planet earth stood by itself and alone hovering in a vast nothingness. Gone was The Wondrous Seventh Level once again, as I had made this trip many times before, and for sure this would be my last, and that is to willing take on a restricted body. As I soon came to hovering above the little planet, I hesitated for a moment, as Rebazar looked at me and smiled, then I knew I would be fine, as we then went down to the surface and the rest is in NUBook Two, which is 'A Journey To RealFreedom!' The time soon came, after being firmly prepared, Paul was given The Rod of Power in approximately 1965. At the time, I was growing up and then going thru my teenage years with Ursha LU as she was teaching me a lot, we were going into many other dimensions together and with Rebazar. As I got thru a lot of drama with my mom and left home at 17, I felt better being on my own. As the years came closer for me to get ready for my time with The RealEvent, Rebazar kept hinting at me to look at what Paul was doing, but for a while I was not interested in studying anything, but I finally did. Then in late 1970, I officially joined Paul's Presentation. During this time, Rebazar showed the two men who would be coming after Paul. At the time, I did not really see what he was sharing with me, as I would just watch as he demonstrated a lot over the years as to what would be coming in my future. It is sometimes hard to explain what takes place on The RealSide, as things are being prepared in a much faster way with a lot more accuracy than we experience here.

While I was with Paul and his Corporation, he had purposely taken on some poison the DarkBrats had given him. Paul knew it was poison, but he was to do this as it was part of the 'Setup' that was to be revealed later with when he was gone. Then Paul was poisoned again at a seminar and it was his time to leave, and rather abruptly as many of the Corporation Members were very shocked. Rebazar was showing me everything that was taking place with Paul's Corporation, as he and Paul met me on The RealSide one night...

"We are getting ready for the next part, Duane, and this will be a Big Test for many of the members to see if they can handle the new and upcoming transformation of Darwin or not. You do not have to be concerned about any of this, as your time will enter when we have gone thru all the steps necessary and all the lessons those who have come this far are prepared for," said Rebazar, as Paul smiled at me.

Several weeks before the Fifth World Wide Seminar in Las Vegas, Nevada, I had met my future wife. I had told her about what I was in to and she agreed to go with me. She began to have RealSide Experiences with Rebazar & Paul, and so she joined the Corporation. As the years went by, the humility Darwin first had soon faded and became a self-adoration, as The Boys were Seeing this taking place. Also, Darwin was starting to embezzle the Corporation funds and he was secretly building a million dollar house for himself in Oregon. At a certain point, Rebazar & The Boys had enough of his silliness and he was politely asked to step aside, which he was not at all happy with, because life was good and he was getting what he wanted from the membership and that was all that mattered to him. So, Rebazar had a very direct talk with him on The RealSide, as he also brought me along to have the experience of this. Rebazar & Paul wanted to teach me how to deal with all the confrontation that would be coming up in my life as I took on The RealPosition with THE ALLIS in the future...

"Darwin, we have asked you directly to step aside and let Harold be known. You are resisting, and because of this we will be stepping in with a lot of your karmic debt if you do not do this Now!" Said Rebazar as he stood face to face with Darwin and looked firmly at him.

Darwin was like a stubborn bratty teenager, because he knew as soon as he let Harold in he would become nothing in the members eyes, so he had devised his own plan in his mind 'Thinking' that he knew more than Life ITSelf. Darwin nodded to Rebazar, then turned and walked away. I watched as a man I really admired became seduced by The Influence to where he was so much more important than what The RealGuides were creating for Everyone. Darwin would have been totally taken care of by The Boys and THE IS, but he wanted those in the Corporation Membership to see him as the 'Master' and and that's what mattered to him the most. Darwin was given the 'Opportunity' to earn and have The Rod of Power, but he never achieved it like Paul had done, as The Boys knew he would be a 'Caretaker' for the time being, even though he took Paul's title instead of creatively creating his own position. There was still some friction on the EarthSide with Harold, but reluctantly, Darwin did announce Harold at the Anaheim, California Seminar. I was in the audience and watched as Darwin made his little speech and then Harold came out like a school boy onto the stage. Darwin's aura was dark and moody as he really did not want to do what he was doing. As he walked off the stage a cloud hovered over him he was taking with him. I could See how he was planning to make his move to try and offset all of this, but he couldn't!

So, now it was Harold's turn to try and Recognize what Darwin was not able to do, SEE THE ALLIS. Here again, Harold is being given the

'Opportunity to Take The Risk' and do what no one else can do, but will he? Harold started off sincere and wanted to stay on a true course, but he still needed a lot of training and RealExperiences to be able to Recognize THE ALLIS, THE ISNESS, Paul had referred to in his writings. Again, Paul started off with the 'God' idea so as to be able to eventually sneak in THE ALLIS. This is what Darwin was shown to gradually do also, but instead of focusing on the TruReality, THE IS, which he still didn't know what IT IS, he kept focusing on what the membership liked about him, and that was his all too charismatic personality, which Darwin had developed listening to the Mate of the Kalaum God, The Influence, and so he had become Possessed and TapLined good. Harold soon became the center of attention as he was announced as The Living Master, and just like Darwin, Harold had been 'Handed' everything Paul had originally created for The Benefit of ALL. And just like Darwin, Harold took on Paul's Title, and so the Sleeping Membership went along with what was taking place, because many people were now Seeing what Darwin had been doing, as it was showing up in their DreamVisions, which it always does.

Almost no one knew that Paul was to purposely leave the earth, so that the formula of Becoming MoreAware would take place and unfold, because the 'Biggest Comparison' for a RealRecognition was about to happen in the near future, even though most of the membership and this world would not altogether be ready for it. But because of what the DarkBrats, the OneWorld Order, had decided hundreds of years ago to do all along with the humans and into this present age, The RealGuides had to continually do something to offset the Over-Kontrol they were implementing on the earth at a rapid pace. The Natural Environment was now being destroyed faster than ever. The Boys kept trying to show Harold what to contribute to what he was here to do, but as SHE showed up, Reptilian Joanny, and took Total Kontrol of what was now the Krone Korporation, Harold soon became just like Darwin, only even moreso. Reptilian Joanny, along with HER Alien Kriminals, who were now in Kontrol of Stage Master HarOld, began TapLining all the MemeberShrimps in their dreams the day SHE married HarOld. Most of the MemberShrimps were totally numb to HER, as so many had become so passive with the funny little stories

HarOld had been telling over the years as SHE was editing them.

I will back up here a bit and go into other TimeFrames that have not been known to the EarthSide of life here. From more than millions of possible candidates, Joanny was chosen by the Kalaum God before SHE even knew it. Joanny was like any other girl, SHE wanted things of course, but to HER, HER needs were special. As the events from what Darwin were doing unfolded, the Kalaum God with his Mistress The Influence were lining up situations for Joanny to take part in and with what Harold was going to enter into, and that is to take Darwin's place as Master of the Corporation. Prior to this, what no one knew is that Harold was summoned by the Kalaum God in his dreams one night. He was escorted to the castle of Kalaum and entered the huge room where the throne of the Reptilian Lord sat. At first, Harold was wondering what was going on in his dream, as Kalaum appeared from behind the giant red curtains and sat on his throne. He looked at the little human, as Harold was a bit amazed as to why he was standing where he was. With a firm voice Kalaum spoke out to Harold...

"Hello earth man. Are you a brave man or just another stupid one?"

Harold was a bit surprised at what Kalaum had said. Harold had met the Kalaum God before when Paul brought him to this very room, but Harold had very little experience with the Managing Lord God. Now, Harold was standing all alone and was being confronted for something he didn't yet know. Kalaum wickedly smiled at Harold and said...

"Well earth man, are you brave or not?"

Intuitively, Harold knew the question had a double meaning, so he wanted to be as witty as he could, and so he said, "A brave man is brave and a stupid man is stupid. I do know the difference, Lord!"

Kalaum laughed and laughed, and then took a few moments to calm down and look upon little Harold. He did a big ugly smile and said...

"Ha ha, we shall see what you are what and what you will become, as it is already written in the stars what you will do little Harold earth boy!"

Suddenly, Harold began to See something more than what he was looking at with the Kalaum God, he could See Kalaum was giving him a hint as to what was coming up in his future. Harold had always liked the idea of prophecy, and what he was Seeing now fascinated him. Kalaum watched as Harold was Seeing his Prophetic Vision. It was a ploy from Kalaum's Mistress, The Influence, to seduce Harold. Harold bought the vision as his own and kept it as a part of his consciousness so that he could use it later. The day did come when Harold took Darwin's place and then made himself 'The Modern Day Prophet.' This was Harold's Real Razors Edge Test, and the results are shown.

Prophecy Now belongs to the Dark Ages, so to speak. It is not that all that IS Seen is prophecy, but The TruReality LifeIS, IS AlwaysNU and Now. A True and Pure Recognition of THE ALLIS, IS The Complete and RealLife every Utun is looking for. What has come to pass as Human History with all the events and purposely 'Slanted' definitions has come and gone and can be used as a reference, but never a Reality for something better in a so-called future. People are always purposely kept in the dark as to What LifeIS, because this is the only way to Kontrol those who are to be subordinate and worship gods. Rebazar & The RealGuides were very Real with what they taught Paul and I (NUBook Three / 'The Real Far Country'). We were taught The RealKnowledge, but Paul was to start off with the 'God' idea, as this would be any easy way for people to relate to what Paul would setup as a RealFoundation for ALL. Rebazar & The Boys ployed the Lord God into accepting what would be presented in his Kingdom on earth, and so he agreed not to overly disturb what Paul was doing at first, because in a way, Paul was referring to Kalaum, so he was pleased. Kalaum kept a sharp eye on what Paul was doing with his Mistress The Influence, as some of Paul's members were heavily TapLined, because they were still very Emotionally Attached to the Old Religious ideas the Old Reptilians had first injected into the Original Humanoids. Human History makes sense once you know what really happened. In the physical realm there are many intersecting dimensions that most people are unaware of and each person will have their experiences here according to what they are aware of. This is where people will say, “Oh, I don't believe that,” which proves their unawareness to The

Whole of Life where Everything IS Possible. Also, the 'idea' of any 'Belief' was a Marketing Ploy to the Dumbed Down Humans, those who worship and pray to the Invented Space Gods from Reptilians.

So, as Harold took over the Corporation, he was given the opportunity to Do Something Real. It became established very fast that the 'Mahanta' idea was also with Harold, but it was not, because originally this idea represented THE ISNESS of the 14th Level, which Harold did not have the awareness for, but he still 'took' Paul's title. Harold had a good intent in the beginning, because he was rather humble and religious, so it fit with what he would start to do. Rebazar & Paul were working with him to get him up to 'speed' so to speak, but at the same time Harold was also enjoying his new fame and fortune he was given, so he became a little sidetracked, but still okay, that is until SHE showed up. SHE, Joanny(Krone / Phoney Baloney Joanny) was a Seductive Witch sent by the Kalaum God and the Reptilian Forces to take Harold down and TapLine him in the Lower ASStral Realm, which SHE had done most effectively. SHE is very good at deceptive disguises, this is why the MemberShrimps have not been able to 'SeeThru' what SHE has been doing for over three decades. Just like the Federal Reserve System and many other Government Kontrolled Businesses that have fooled people for hundreds of years, Joanny has done the very same thing with the blindside of the physical body and how immature it is. People are taught to 'Think' they really know something when in fact they really do not. Those who 'Think' they are the smartest people are usually the furthest from any such thing.

Most of the MemberShrimps are Emotionally Attached to the ideas of masters, gods, initiations and titles. They are not mature enough to See the fallacy of what has been 'created' in Creation, nor have they been paying attention to how Creation really works, and it is not what has been 'Marketed' from the Old Belief Systems of Kontrol. Nature, right in front of everyone 'Demonstrates' What IS Always Real Now, but very few people pay attention to this, and also what is Seen Thru all of what is demonstrated. THE ALLIS, becomes something that is not at all understood by this little world, as IT has nothing to do with Creation, where people have been taught that Creation is the ultimate and there is nothing else. This is the Ploy of Maya or what I call The Influence, which is not very well known by the Political, Religious or Spiritual Systems in The TruSense. So, from the time Paul was here with The Rod of Power, to this very present moment, which THE ALLIS, IS, THE NUWAVIS THE NUMAN IS NOW. All that has taken place before this very moment is Ancient History and nothing more than Old Memories people emotionally hang on to. Free Will can be the biggest burden when it is not properly understood, which it is not by most of this world. It is all about 'Choice' and what is decided. The masses have been taught to rationalize, reason out and logically calculate what LifeIS, and none of this IS What LifeIS, but what It isn't.

I am on My Own Journey with THE ALLIS. This is where Rebazar Tarzs, Paul Twitchell & The RealGuides stand, but very few will See this Now. What I am Sharing here is a very brief explanation of so much more that has taken place and even more that will take place. Anyone can decide whatever they want, but it has nothing to do with the Whole of Life, THE IS, just because a person 'Thinks' so. The beginning of time here is not at all recorded as it really happened, and the 'Biblical' silliness and 'Other So-Called Holey Stuff' was invented by the World Reptilian Kontrollers to herd people like cattle and to use them as slaves for lifetimes. The same Kontrolling Factors are at work all over this Korporation World of chasing printed money by those who use people as play things for their own selfish purposes. The United States has marketed itself into something it was and no longer is, and is owned by the Ratican in Rome, and is the biggest deception with the 'Holey Rollers' who rule the earth. They are the Reptilians, and they do not care for humans at all, only as slaves and dogs. People can 'Pretend' whatever they want in the LA LA Land of this world, but everything here changes. I See huge amounts of people on The RealSide panicking and running into nowhere, because they do not know where to go with themselves, because they will not take the time and have the patience for RealGuidance and a RealEducation. I am 'Simply Reporting The News' as I have experienced it! I am not a master and never claimed to be one. I was asked by Rebazar & The RealGuides to Be THE NUMAN, and this is what I am doing Now, as I LUV this RealAdventure and The NUChallenge! Have Fun Deciding!

MEMBRAINS WORSHIPING KRONEE

There becomes a scream in the night..."AAAAAHHH... What did I just dream?" Yelled Harold within himself, as he looked over at his wife as she was still sleeping. Harold was sweating as he laid stiff in the bed. He was to embark on an adventure that he could never have imagined to happen, but it already has for him, as he is right in the middle of it and he cannot See it. None of us really know what Life has in store for us until we Take The Risk, and so it is with Harold in this Time-Frame as he is about to embark into his future. Can it be that Life is as simple as we try and make it? Of course not! Creation is a Huge Challenge to get thru, and most people do not know there is so much more to Life than just Creation. Harold's dream with the Kalaum God, he is now facing the challenge of his life, and that is to Recognize what will be coming into his life... SHE! Human History may or may not record what I am Reporting and Sharing here, but no difference, because most people will stay asleep for a long time into the future. Now we go to the Kalaum God Palace and what the God of Men is doing and seeing, as Harold has woken from his dream...

"Ha, Ha, Ha, let's see if the little fool can do what he 'thinks' he can," said Kalaum as his Mistress The Influence watched with him.

Kalaum and The Influence were making plans for Harold, just like the OneWorld Order Reptilians have done for centuries with the unaware people of earth. It is the adventure of the Kalaum God to keep people worshiping and praying as an activity for those who have not Become MoreAware of The TruReality LifeIS, THE ALLIS. Kalaum has no reference beyond his kingdom, and so it is his nature to hold people to his level of awareness. He is a lonely god with an unlimited amount of Funny Followers, just like those who vote for the politicians that 'Think' life on earth will be better if people vote for a person who says 'Pretty Words' to an onlooking unaware audience. Who are the worshipers, prayers and voters of these people? Someone does know, because they keep creating situations that Kontrol them into being stupid. After thousands of years of Brutal Barbaric History, these same unaware people keep 'Agreeing' to the routines they have already been thru, yet most people make no effort to free themselves from the Silly Restrictions they have worshiped for untold lifetimes. The Gods of Men and their Earthly Korporations (EK) keep telling people to... "Love Everything and all will be well. God will take care of you and Jeezo will return and clean up the big mess all of you have made!" I like the distorted and deformed sense of humor the Authoritarian's have, those who Fluoridate the water supply to keep the masses dah and stupid, secretly do the ChemTrails in the sky, building microwave towers almost everywhere for Mind Kontrol, create GMO TechFood to contaminate all of us, use the Big HAARP Machine to blast the earth and create earthquakes, change the weather and disintegrate people, vaccinate the public to have autism workers in the Fema Camps for the Kontrolling Korporations. Yes, all this and so much more will be taken care of by those who 'Just Love Everything!' And as we have seen in Human History with all the Takeovers and Purposely Planned Tyranny, "It is Not Working!" What I am saying here is that what has been secretly created as a Definite Destruction Deal is The Greatest Comparison as to what 'Not to Do.' Those who have have The Real PerSeeving of THE ALLIS, will have the opportunity like never before to See what all others will not. Okay, on with this RealAdventure...

At some point in time and space, and this can be verified with the local authorities, that Harold got his legal divorce and he married Joanny. All this is fine and good, as I have gone thru the same experiences many times over. I am not getting personal here, this is just part of the story others want to know. So, SHE enters the picture, which SHE already has a Predetermined Plan from the Reptilian Queen in the Lower ASStral Realm to where we will now go with what took place before the lovely wedding ceremony between both of them on earth...

We have to go deep into the gloom of the murky ASStral Arena that most people do not want to even consider, accept those that like heavy metal music and devilish symbols tattooed all over themselves. Here you will find the headquarters of the Reptilian Alien Invaders that have made 'deals' with some of the Religious and Political Kontrollers on the many RoundWorlds in the Physical Realm. These Kontrolling Kreatures actually eat the little humans like humans eat GMO Doritos. As we move thru all the yukky glokk and smelly gruesome odors of knarled formations, we finally come to where the Queen HESELF is hiding. SHE is a Scaly Reptilian Deformity with grotesque features from all the lifetimes of battling and murder and having a really bad attitude. What SHE represents is what is seen on the surface world of the Restricting Religious Regimes, those that Totally Kontrol all the RoundWorlds in disguise of something genuine, but the very radical opposite fact is definitely so. There really can be no accurate assault of what should be narrowed to and directly accused as to the very lowest of all implementations on physical embodiments ever, as it is with the Reptilians who Rule the Earthly Korporations in the name of their Lizard Headed God, Kalaum, Lord God of All Invented Doctrines and all that can and will be stolen from others and possessed by him.

Here in the unmistakeable gloom of what would be a 'Worst Nightmare Scenario' for anyone, little miss Joanny stood naked in front of the Reptilian Queen, as SHE was taken from HER body and transported in HER Astral Form, so as to start a Nightmare Journey SHE would never forget! Just like in Harold's dream, Joanny was to confront what SHE would be putting HERSELF into, because of the desires SHE had already displayed to Kalaum and the Queen. Like Harold, Joanny was rather alarmed as to where SHE was now standing. It was like a really bad gruesome scene from the movie, 'Rosemary's Baby' that Joanny was actually standing in the middle of. For Joanny, even with all HER fondest desires now coming face to face with HER, SHE was finding all this actuality hard to accept and understand. For a moment, SHE was ready to pass out and get HER mind out of this horrible place. But then the Queen snapped at HER...

“Wake up Joanny! You really are here even though it may seem like a dream to you, what you are Seeing is all you have secretly desired. I can See you, but just like little Harold, you cannot See yourself and where your desire to have power and rule others has led you. You want 'Power!' You want to Rule!' Well, this is it! When you see the

President of a country standing in front of the crowd and looking so noble with his fine suit on and the nicely created symbol of his official office stamped on the front of the podium he is saying his Pretty Words from, you 'Think' in your little mind that that is what You want, don't You? Yes You Do! But, what you do not See with your physical eyes is what really is behind and supporting the 'Front' of what the One-Dimensionals are seeing and not seeing. Your life has come to this, and this is what you have always wanted, and now you are Seeing it as it really is... Raw Power of the Kontrolling Order! From many you have been chosen to be in the best of all positions to seize what the Reptilian Kingdom has always wanted to posses, 'The Rod of Power!" My Lord Kalaum God has always been so intrigued with its secrecy, because on the earth it is 'The Secret Societies' we Kontrol that rule the earth with all the agreement we have from the unaware."

"Do you see people voting for their Political figures if they knew who they really are? No! Not at all! It is the 'Deception' they are listening to, to and placing their bets on as they vote for the candidates of their choice, but actually not of their choice. Both sides, that of DemoRats and Reptilikons are from The Skull & Bones Secret Society. All the elections are fixed, especially with the technology of today. Whether people vote or not does not matter, because the 'Reptilian House' always wins. This is the way of the worlds in time and space. People are used as servants and slaves to build and maintain what we want for ourselves, that is why we originally created them. Like mice they have flourished out of control, so it is time to exterminate billions of them like the pests they are. ChemTrails, Vaccines, Microwaves from Cell Phones, GMO TechFood, Entertainment, Propaganda and all the things we love, and especially the 'Love God' idea, which emotionally binds people to their ASStral Bodies and then we TapLine the hell out of them! Or I should say, we suck the life out of them and then bring them into our hell. Fear is our purpose, up front and straight out Fear! But of course we have so many ways to disguise Fear for the unaware to agree to and completely accept as part of their nature, that is what we want them to 'Think' anyhow. You will come to know all you need to in a very short time, because you are a very cleaver girl, Joanny, this is why we picked you from thousands of others, you are the best! Simply pay attention to what I will be teaching you," said the Queen.

Joanny stood naked and silent as SHE looked straight at the Queen and listened to every word very closely. It was very true with HER, all of this was so much more than what SHE was expecting, but because Joanny was more focused on what SHE wanted than what things here looked like, SHE was Seeing the potential for HERSELF. The Kalaum God wanted HER, which seemed like a big deal, a type of honor to be picked from all the others. Joanny could understand some of the Fear the Queen was talking about and the rest of what SHE needed to know would come as SHE gained more experience, as SHE asked...

"What really is The Rod of Power? I have heard of it and I have asked others in the Corporation, but no one seems to really know."

"Ha ha, you are such a child like all humans are, and you will soon be Reptilian completely! The Rod of Power, as Paul Twitchell referred to it, is something we have studied for centuries, as we have known of the Strange Being Rebazar Tarzs and seen him for the longest time, and with others like him. We cannot as of yet figure him or the others out, but we will, we always do, because there is always a 'flaw' in everyone. He possesses The Power Rod and will be giving it in trust to Harold, your new husband in Wedlock," said the Queen smiling.

Joanny was very intrigued by all of what the Queen was saying. SHE loved the 'takeover' idea of Harold, who was a dweeb of sorts with a homely wife. Joanny knew SHE could be very seductive and have fun with Her new job, that of taking down the man the members of the Corporation would be trusting. At the same time, Rebazar & The Boys knew all of this and so much more of what was being planned, and they could easily See the outcome of what would be decided. But, as Life must go on, Harold was to be given The Real Opportunity, because it was his place to be where he was at during this time and do whatever he would do. Rebazar knew what would take place, as he told me and so did Paul. I cannot even write about or explain all

The RealSide Experiences I have had that has led up to this event and all that most people will never come close to knowing. It Now seems to be the time to have some fun with continuing this adventure and going over what I have not put in The AdventurIS Series. Kronee Joanny has done so many things SHE does not even come close to realizing HERSELF. SHE, in her own mind 'Thinks' SHE knows what SHE is doing, but SHE is Kontrolled by what SHE is deciding. Until a person has The TruActuality of Recognizing THE ALLIS, and Seeing how Creation of itself works in accordance with The TruRecognition of ALL That IS, then one will move from 'idea to idea' and use other ideas to support the creation and ideas they dream up. What I am explaining here makes so much more sense than chasing false power.

Rebazar & Paul shared this experience of Joanny with me, along with others I will be writing about as this adventure continues. Joanny HERSELF was not aware of this taking place, because HER Earthly Side would have probably had a heart attack from the Fear and Fright. The same goes for Harold, as he has had many experiences that were shown to me, so that I would have the Recognition of what Darwin and Harold are not able to Recognize with THE ALLIS. THE NUWAVIS like nothing that has happened on this earth before, but only so many people will Recognize what I am Presenting Now. The TruReality IT IS, can only be expressed with THE NUMAN from this 'Place in Life' at this time and Seen by those who PerSeeve the combination of Creation and THE ALLIS. Paul gave the outer and inner initiations, and this is what Life 'was' at the time and what was to take place. The 'routines' he used are no longer workable, as they have actually become forms of Kontrol and Manipulation. The Reality LifeIS, is where only YU can determine Your RealPosition. People have been 'babysat' for eons, but no more. That is, for those who Recognize they do not need masters and the Kontrolling Korporations of the Physical Realm. Each of us decides what our life will be in Life, but because of the process we must each go thru, we also have to deal with the Restrictions of Creation and the Five PsycBodies, which most people are only aware they are what they have determined as human. From this physical vehicle and a mind that only knows what it can absorb from its surroundings, The RealU has the challenge of bringing into focus Something So Real as to not be known here at all according to what creatively exists, and especially when people only have distorted information and propaganda to try and sort out who they really are. THE NUWAVIS HERE NOW. This is The NUNowniss.

As Joanny stood naked, the Queen continued to dictate to HER...

"You have a direct order from Kalaum himself, and that is to take over what Harold will have and to also take charge and Kontrol of the HU. The HU Word and the vibrations from it are very disturbing to us. We cannot penetrate certain areas in the physical and Astral Realm with all those using it. We have rehearsed the masses to use the AUM Word for centuries, which brings the unaware to the feet of Kalaum and many times his brother Jot, to where we can TapLine almost anyone. With the 'Emotional Love' idea and that god will take care of everything for people brings them into a passive submission to where TapLining is very easy. My race of Reptilians feeds off the reactive emotions of those creatures we want to posses, and this is why the basis of any Political or Religious System we have set up is based upon Fear, even though we profess it to be love we are sharing. It will also be your job to make sure the HU Word becomes useful to us instead of exposing what we have built for eons. How you will do this is very simple, you will begin to implement the worship and praying to the Kalaum God. By worshiping and praying to a god, the emotional bodies of the members will be easily TapLined. The Real UNUversal Guides, which you are not aware of, which Harold and you will refer to as 'masters' have their missions with some unknown reality we are not familiar with. There has never been a time when anyone of our agents has been able to identify what they relate to and what it is."

"Also, Rebazar is training someone else who may show up in your future, but we do not know who this is yet or if it will even happen, as we will do our best and so will you to fool Harold and the membership, and we will handle Rebazar and those he knows. Once you have Harold seduced, the others in the headquarters will be easy, because most of them are already passive and willing to become worshipers and followers of Kalaum. It will be the 'Front' you will built to convince others and how you direct Harold as to what he should be doing. Let him be the little master he wants to be and play up to him. He has been a secluded person for the most part, and what he will be experiencing with all the adoration will take his attention to the mission he 'Thinks' he is on. The Reptilians work from the Vatican in Rome, as the Popes have all been Reptilians, accept those that were killed and were given the chance like you are now to work with Kalaum. I have been around since we first set foot on the earth and other planets. Paul actually wrote about me in one of his books, but he didn't go into detail, because he doesn't want to scare people as to what is really taking place on the earth. He wanted to quietly setup his foundation with those who taught him. Many of us tried time and again to get him to see things our way, but he was very stubborn and showed no interest. No matter, with you Kontrolling Harold, we will have what we want, because we are very, very patient," SHE said.

Joanny soon came silently back to HER body as though nothing had happened. Just like in Rosemary's Baby, SHE knew something took place and SHE was not aware of this, but the 'Cause' of what SHE would be doing was set into motion without Her even having to see it, because SHE had already agreed to it. The Mate of Kalaum, The Influence, now had its way with Joanny without HER being fully aware of it. This is how desire works with those who do not See what they are wanting. As the time came for Joanny to make HER move for Harold under the orders of the Queen, SHE quickly took advantage and it became so. The human mind is so frail, and all those who were with the Corporation at the time were agreeable to this arrangement, accept for one. As SHE set HERSELF up and into motion, the HU Word became saturated with a blend of Reptilian Vibration that was like a drug almost no one noticed. As Joanny became physically bonded to Harold, he became intoxicated with the Main TapLines from the Queen HERSELF. Even Joanny did not See this, as HER attention was always on the 'Takeover' process, which SHE has been excellent at. Kalaum and the Queen have become very proud of HER.

KARMA IS NOT A KURSE

What is know as 'The Law of Karma' is really 'Cause & Effect' to learn from. The Process of Karma is in Creation, and is the 'Opposites' like good and bad, right and wrong, all of us experience while we are in a Material Body, along with the four other Unseen Bodies we have. The 'idea' of Karma some people have is that it is more like a Kurse than a learning process to Become MoreAware. This is understandable, and this is why so many in their own way try and rebel against Life or the Invented Gods, who are actually the TapLining Reptilians that have forced people to 'Believe' in them. The Law of Karma is in the Five PsycRealms of Creation. THE ALLIS, The TruReality LifeIS, has set into motion a 'Simulation' of Life with bodies and minds that have all kinds of emotional reactions and baggage to deal with. It really is a burden to deal with the Cause and Effects of Creation, and especially for those who know nothing about THE ALLIS, and only the limited ideas of religions, politics and gods. The Simulation of Creation has a huge impact with the body, emotions and mind of every person on this planet and anywhere in the PsycRealms. Until a person Becomes MoreAware and Wakes Up to The TruReality, they will stay unaware.

LifeIS ALL About Becoming MoreAware, and the Law of Karma plays the role of providing a 'Comparison,' but only when YU WakeUp to THE ALLIS, otherwise YU are at the mercy of not knowing how Cause and Effect really work. When YU have The RealConnection to The SoundLight Reality LifeIS with The Real UNUversal Guides, then YU will Become MoreAware and 'Recognize' a much bigger picture for yourself than just the 'Human' idea. But, until YU 'Take The Risk' to WakeUp from Your 'LA LA Land' life here, and See what is really happening all around YU, and especially with Your Mind and The RealU, Your RealAwareniss, YU will continue into more episodes and drama with future lifetimes on this planet or others. Karma has a Real Purpose as an Essential to 'Recognize' and then to 'PerSeeve' The TruReality LifeIS, THE ALLIS. The Journey to RealFreedom begins when YU Recognize The RealU, moreso than any Invented God, YU are ALL Life ITSelf, but YU must See this for YourSelf with The NU-U.

FREE YOURSELF FROM TAPLINING

TapLining has been around for longer than you can imagine and it has been very well hidden from almost all the public. I know it is hard for a person to even consider that it exists, but it really does and there is a lot more to TapLining than meets the eyes of the physical body. You have TapLines, but you cannot See them with your eyes, and so you must learn to See them and Recognize what they are, starting in Your DreamVisions. The best way to start is to do The NU-U Sessions as explained in The NUBooks and is now on Facebook. When you do The NU-U Sessions you are starting to have The RealConnection to The SoundLight Reality of THE ALLIS. THE ALLIS, IS The TruReality LifeIS. THE IS or THE ALLIS, has nothing to do with the Gods of Man, which have been invented from the minds of those who Kontrol the people of this planet. You can accept this or not, it is all your choice, and in the same instant you can learn to prove What IS Real Now to yourself, and only YU, The RealU can do this when YU decide.

LifeIS so much bigger and better than YU will ever imagine with as many lifetimes here as YU can possibly have. There are Endless Dimensions and Levels to Life that are unseen by your senses. Here is where YU have to BE a Real RiskTaker and decide to do what YU have never done before, or YU will stay the same as YU always have, unaware and the Effect of everything here. TapLining is part of the Purposely Planned Procedures to get people to accept 'fear' as their basis for living. Because fear is purposely hidden in so many things, those who Kontrol others can easily inject TapLines into a person's Astral Body without them ever knowing it, thus many people become manipulated according to the Kontrolling Systems of Politics, Religion, Spiritual Paths & their TapLining Presidents, Kings, Queens, Masters and Mates. Everything on earth is based upon 'Agreement' and as long as people keep 'Agreeing' to the same Old Restricted Routines of being Kontrolled, then The ALLNatural Environment that Supports ALL of US will continue to be affected here. And those who want to keep Kontrolling others and getting them to 'Agree' to More Restrictions will be back many times over until they do WakeUp to What IS Real Now!

THE STUPIDIANS

“It is not that people are Stupid, but many people do act the part very well!” DUANE THE GREAT WRITER 1776. Life on earth has become what it has, because of the choices each person has made. Some may 'Think' it is their god making the choices and that what we are experiencing here is all a Big Test. Others 'Believe' it is the work of the Devil, and that most people like the Devil more than they do the Invented Gods of Man. Some like to blame the Political System for almost everything and being so corrupt and uncaring. These are a few of the silly things some people carry with them as their answer to what is taking place here. Today, we are experiencing a huge amount of pollution and poisoning that the Dumbed Down Public seems to 'Think' appeared from nowhere, as many people do not at all pay attention to what is really taking place on the planet they live on. You already have all the answers for everything you need, but it where you are placing your 'Focus and Intent' that matters, but then again, you have 'Agreed' to be taught by those who have invented the Systems of Deception, and so this is where you are with everyone else today.

And of course, you may not care about any of what the world is going thru and dealing with and what will happen as events continue onward into an unknown future. Each one of us decides what is taking place here and it is all about 'Agreement' and what we each individually decide to do and how we See the outcome. From all that has taken place, it makes a lot more sense to do what was being done before life on earth has become what it has Now. The masses have accepted the idea of 'Fear' more than anything else from those who are afraid of losing their Kontrol over others. So, it is as that famous whoever said, “Stupid is as Stupid has already done!” People are Being Stupid right in front of themselves, yet they are basically not at all concerned. Most of the population walks around saying, “Why doesn't anybody do something about all this?” Does this make any sense? People talking to people making no sense. They do have time for entertainment and not doing anything about what they have done. Read My NUBooks and Learn 'Something Wonderful' for YourSelf!!

TAPLINING FROM ALIENS

UFO's have been a mystery to the masses, because of all the 'Cover Ups' by Government Officials around the world. Today, there is more information being given to the public and also by those who are brave enough to investigate what most people are too afraid to. UFO's have been a common experience for so many people throughout Human History and have been documented over and over, yet the 'officials' keep denying this to the point to where people are 'seeing things' that are not really there, which is really their Game of Kontrol. All of us are in the same Life and we can all See what is really taking place with anything or anyone. Your DreamVisions is an excellent way of Seeing what most people pay no attention to. The 'Average Person' wants to simply live their LA LA Land Life here and that's it, which is their right to do so, not knowing they will always be the Effect of everything in Creation until they learn to Become MoreAware and Recognize themselves as a Free Being of RealLight. TapLining is something that has been very well hidden for thousands of years and is Now coming to the surface as Duane The Great Writer makes this known so all See it.

The Invented Kontrolling Governments of the earth have been 'Doing Business as Usual' with many types of Alien Visitors for eons. The Dumbed Down and Unaware Public has had no idea that this has been going on right underneath them, as there are tunnels all thru the earth where many of the Aliens live Right Now. There are many people who have encounters with Aliens, but they are usually too afraid to say anything, and especially if they are confronted by Government Officials to keep quite. On YouTube many people, even those who once worked for the Kontrolling Governments, have made Videos and Documentaries about Aliens and what they are really doing here. The 'Average Citizen' is only interested in Texting and Football Games and eating popcorn as a way of life here, not realizing there is so much more going on that is effecting them. Duane The Great Writer suggests to Test The NU-U Sessions and Watch Your DreamVisions and YU will begin to have RealGuidance and a Real Education as to what is really taking place here and in Your Dreams.

TAPLINING INKORPORATED

First off, I would like to sincerely thank Reptilian TapLining Phoney Baloney Joanny and her sidekick (and SHE does kick him around) Stage Master Harry (alias 'Doorstop Harry' and other references I have not yet discovered) of the Kroney TapLining Korporation, also known as EEEkonkon. Also, I would like to include some of HER friends who are also Reptilians... The Federal Reserve Korporation, the Black Pope, Washington DC, and far too many others to mention. Thank You, Thank You all for making 'An Adventure Like No Other' for me to experience and write about, this has been so terrific, as I like to Share. Since SHE married Harry and came to the Korporation of Master Harry, SHE has done what very few have even dared to 'Think' about or do, but of course with the entire Reptilian Alien Nation of Intergalactic TapLiners backing HER to takeover Master Harry and the MemberShrimps, SHE has confidence like no one else. Sound just too fantastic to fathom or 'believe' as all good Kalaum God Lovers would say? Well, there is a lot more, and as YU the Reader 'Take The Risk' and find out 'What IS Real Now,' YU will discover that Reptilian Baloney Joanny is also hooked up with the OneWorld Order that rules the planet earth. Yes, this is a Real WakeUp Call with what is taking place with so many Korporations of this world, as they have been setup by Ratican City in Rome for centuries. This world is just Now discovering what has been taking place right in front of everyone by those who created and own the Monetary System that pays for all the tyranny the people of this planet have been experiencing for so many lifetimes. Miss Phoney Joanny and HER Korporate Kroneees have completely taken over Master Harry and the Numb MemberShrimps.

As Stage Master Harry steps out from behind the curtains to say his 'Pretty Political Words' (probably the same curtains Joanny and him hide behind and TapLine people in their Astral Bodies in the Astral Realm), the announcer signifies his title, which he took from Paul Twitchell, as Harry claims to have the same or even greater awareness than Paul. The best part of this whole 'Show' is, YU can be shown 'What IS Real Now' from Rebazar Tarzs and The Real

UNUversal Guides in Your DreamVisions, that is if YU have the courage to do so. TapLining is an ancient device created by the Reptilian Aliens, the same Aliens that are in many of the Old Scriptures and Holey Books people have been emotionally intimidated by for lifetimes. Like the Walking Dead (kind of like people texting and not watching where they are going), the masses have been 'Bred to Obey' what is fed to them with 'Pretty Words, Marketing Ploy and GMO TechFood' to name a few examples. Most people have never heard of TapLining, because it has been hidden in the vaults at Ratican City for centuries, and only a very select few of Kontrolling Reptilians know about it and how it works, as they have been doing TapLining for thousands of years on people all over the planet earth.

The governments of this world have been practicing Astral Projection, Remote Viewing, Time Travel and other scientific mediums for many centuries, and experimenting with those who are unaware of what is taking place. This also accounts for all the Alien Abductions that have happen for decades, as many of the government officials have made deals with the Reptilians and given their 'okay' to take people and use them as 'Guinea Pigs' for Alien Experiments. TapLining is one of the easier forms of Emotional and Mental Kontrol the Aliens use for the sake of feeding off their emotional stimulation's, like people who are having the sensations of sex, as an example. The TapLines are placed in the person's Astral, Causal and Mental Bodies, mainly that of the Astral Body, and hooked into the backside of the person so they do not see or know what is taking place. What will soon occur from this is backaches, sore muscles, spasms, diseases and even cancers until death. The Reptilians will suck a person dry as long as they keep 'Agreeing' to the Emotional Attachments they have come to know from the Political and Religious Systems and other TapLining Kontrolling Korporations. The Main TapLiner is the Kalaum God, who is the God of all those who Worship and Pray to any God. I suggest to do a lot of investigating and to practice The NU-U Sessions and Watch Your DreamVisions. YU can be shown how to rid yourself of Restricting TapLines, because they do have an effect on your health and well being and unnecessary karma. Take The Risk, YU will like yourself!

WELCOME TO LA LA LAND

From hundreds of miles far out in space as you look upon the planet earth, it looks to be such a peaceful and interesting place. Suddenly you are descending down towards it and looking forward to another lifetime of what you have been through so many times before, and you still want to keep experiencing what seems to be an almost endless succession of relationships you want to continue with. Before you enter the earth's atmosphere, you can still recall all the love and passion from some of your previous lifetimes on the earth along with other planets you have been on. You don't want to look at the hard times and all the heartaches and hard work it took you to finally get somewhere in those previous lives. No, you want to 'Think' that this life will be better and you will finally find what you have always been looking for, which you have no idea what it is, because of all the times you have tried to find it and you never did. Now, you are very close to your entrance into someone's body to make a new body for yourself. You still have the chance to change directions and head off somewhere else, but you decide to go for it and see what comes of this life.

Suddenly, your are five years old, then fifteen, then twenty five! Wow, this really is how fast things happen here. Just look at yourself Now, Yes YOU the Reader! YOU are all of a sudden whatever age you are Now and it really did not take that long, did it? Well, here you are again and doing what you have for countless lifetimes and have Now forgotten. As you look around this world you kind of like what you see. You might be one of those who was raised by a nice family, and probably religious, and you have a good job and maybe a house of your own with a mate and kids. If so, you are the typical person who is just 'going along' with what is taking place here and living in your own LA LA LAND. You do not See that this place is a 'House of Mirrors' as you keep 'Agreeing' to what you and others are creating. It is not 'good or bad' what you are experiencing here, it is Creation! But, you do not really know what Creation is, do you? You 'Think' you know, and you have possibly read a lot and even went to school and college, but you still really do not know where you are and why you are here, do you? Again, you 'Think' you know because you are an educated person and you can dress yourself, drive a car, make house payments and work at your 9 to 5 boring job and imagine a great future and retirement for yourself, yes you can do all this! But, can you really survive what is really taking place here? You 'Think' you can, because you know how to use your Cell Phone and 'text' to all your friends and family, as you are bored and have nothing else to do.

You are in LA LA LAND! YES! YOU really are here in LA LA Land, but you still do not Recognize who YOU, The RealU, really are and why you are here. Even though this physical life can be hard at times you still like it here, that is as long as it does not get too hard for you, then you may start to consider other things as so many people have, like suicide. You know this is an option for you, but you do not want to go there, because you do not know what will happen when you do. So for Now, we will just stick with your so-called Happy Life in LA LA Land. You may be like most people who do not realize that the microwave oven you use is giving you radiation and carcinogenic food and your Cell Phone does the same thing. Also, most of the so-called food you are buying and eating is GMO TechFood, which kills Bees and Butterflies and poisons the earth. This is just the start of what you will WakeUp to with what is taking place on the earth Now. There is a lot more going on in your house and you can learn to discover what that is. So for now, when you go outside you will see long streaks in the sky, they are ChemTrails. The OneWorld Order that rules the planet is purposely spraying the populations of this world to get rid of at least five billion people. Again, as you do your research you will learn whay this is happening, but of course the governments who are doing this will tell you that those are 'jet trails' and nothing to be concerned about. It is Your Choice to 'Agree' or find out for yourself.

I am just getting started here, so pay close attention. As you go to start your car, just like at least five billion others, along with those who fly aircraft and have boats and ships on 'YOUR OCEANS' you are purposely poisoning yourself and others. This is because this is what you have been trained to purposely do! You may 'believe or Think' in your 'Educated Militarized Mind' that this cannot possibly be so, but it really is, and YOU keep 'Agreeing' to it. Then you drive your car, which is a huge liability all its own, but you do not see it this way, as it is more of a 'pleasure' in LA LA Land to have a car and contribute to all the pollution. At wherever you work, which you probably 'Think' is a good place or not so good, whatever, you do your job not realizing that your job is actually contributing to the demise of the planet. But of course, your job and the business you work for, or if you are in your own business, is just like any other business that is doing the same as you are, so all is fine, because you are in LA LA Land, and all is good.

After a hard day at the office you want to relax and possibly watch the 6 O'Crock News to see whats going on with the world. The TV Stuff of today does look really good and those who produce what they do for television do a great job marketing you and also adding 'Subliminal Messages' to almost everything. These same messages are also in the movies and even the animated films that are popular. The Crock News is purposely 'slanted' to make you feel good about certain things and to react emotionally to other events, because those who do this want your support for their products or their World Kontrol Ideals. You always have a choice, but then again you do not want to be different from your friends, family and neighbors, so you will usually Agree to almost anything everyone else is doing. You like Your LA LA Land Life and for the most part, you want it to stay the same and just keep going as it has, especially if your parents worked all their life and have a good retirement, you want the same as they have. All of this does seem so nice and cozy and you have a right to it, this is real. But, as you are going thru your daily routine, just like Gigantic Termites, the OneWorld Order that rules this planet is doing Funny Things you do not know about 24 hours a day everyday, and they have been doing this for hundreds of years right in front of everyone here, but very few people are able to See what they are really doing, because they are too afraid to See. You always have a choice to See or not to See. It is all up to you to WakeUp to what is really going on here or Stay Asleep for more unconscious lifetimes and continue to be the effect of everything around you. I suggest you test what I am presenting Now!

ASTRAL BODY TAPLINNING

Most of this Dumbed Down and asleep world is not aware that most people are being Astrally TapLined in their dreams. Astral TapLining is as ancient as the Pyramids and has always been kept as a big secret, because this is how the masses are Kontrolled unconsciously in their sleep. While people are awake and aware of what is taking place on the earth it is a bit harder to fool people, as the Political, Religious and Spiritual Systems have done for ages. What I call the REPSystems (Religious, Educational, Political & SciFi Social) have dominated most people for centuries and even longer. I am actually being kind here, because it is a lot worse than most people can imagine or even want to know. Those in Kontrol of the Governments, Korporations, Queens and their Kings, Dictators, Authoritarians, Presidents, Masters, Gurus, and so many more, are basically of the Reptilian Order, as they were the first creatures on this planet. They created Humanoids as slaves. You can read about this in the coming pages, 'IN THEE BEGINNING'

Astral TapLining is very commonly known by Religious and Political Korporations, as it has been part of their Satanic Rituals for untold centuries. 'Skull & Bones' is an old time favorite for most of the World's Diplomatic Rulers. Today, many Korporations use various TapLining Techniques, as they market their products and seduce people to work for them and buy the useless junk they are selling. One of the biggest businesses is 'Selling Pretty Words' to people who 'Think' they are getting some kind of 'divine knowledge' which they are not. The average person on earth is taught to 'chase printed money' and establish a home and lifestyle on this planet. The masses are marketed into 'Thinking' that the earth is the only place in Life there is, so people had better make the most of their life while they are here. It is the Reptilian Rulers, such as those Presidents in the US, who have had the most current Kontrol over the Purposely Dumbed Down Mass Populations. This Physical Dimension is like a Cyber Space Vacuum that has been created for certain species to have psychological sway over most unaware people. The Ratican in Rome, Italy, basically heads the World Systems of KalKontrol. It is 'The Nest' for the Ruling

Religious Reptilians and they spy on everyone and mainly use the US Government (Washington DC / a Private Korporation) as their Political Puppets. Virtually all the US Presidents have been Masons and Illuminati Members. The World Kontrol of the 'Certain Few' is very dominate and this is why the earth is so polluted and poisoned, because in this day and age the Reptilian Rulers want to get rid of at least Five Billion people for using 'Their' resources. YouTube and the Internet are a good source for research and also Your DreamVisions.

The past and present Presidents, some of Congress, some Movie Stars, the Queen of England, to name a few, are Reptilian Rulers, and there are so many more, plus other Outer Space Aliens on the earth at this time. There Alien Creatures have huge technology, moreso than what the public sees. The Reptilian Aliens (RA) are doing abductions, sacrifices and experiments on humans for their DNA and other uses. All of this and so much more has taken place for centuries without most of the public ever knowing it. Today, with the arrival of Paul Twitchell in 1965, and being given what this world knows nothing about, The Rod of Power from Rebazar Tarzs, Paul brought in a NUEra, which is just Now being Realized & Recognized. Paul started his presentation off with the 'spiritual' idea and the Gods of Man, which were created by the Original Reptilians to make the Humanoids 'dogs' to their Alien Masters. Dog spelled backwards is God. This was all purposely done back in time before there were any historians writing about such events. As time went on and the Humanoids populated this world, the Reptilians created doctrines such as the Bible and other writings to psychologically enslave people with their emotions and mind. This is very evident in today's world, yet very few can 'See' this as it is taking place right in front of them. Paul Twitchell was killed by the Reptilians, because he was giving out too much knowledge, which he would have brought more forward if he had stayed longer.

Rebazar Tarzs & The Real UNUversal Guides, who played their roles as 'masters' while Paul was here, then chose another man, Darwin Gross. Darwin was taught very rapidly to take the reins of what Paul had created, but he eventually fell victim to 'The Influence,' a very seductive reality in the PsycRealms from the Kalaum Reptilian God. The next man was brought in by Rebazar & The Boys, Harold Klemp. Like Darwin, Harold was given the opportunity to 'Recognize' The Rod of Power and what 'IT IS,' but soon after he was chosen, Kalaum sent The Influence to take over Joanny, Harold's new wife. SHE was very open to being Kontrolled by Kalaum and his Mistress, The Influence. SHE has brought in the Reptilian Kontrol over the MemberShrimps who are so unaware as to what is really taking place Now. SHE is the Main TapLiner for the Reptilian Influence, as SHE works with the One World Order who Kontrols the earth from Ratican City in Rome. SHE has been TapLining people for more than 30 years, and this is why people are ill, have back problems, and are even dying of cancers. SHE Kontrols Master HarOld, as he is HER Puppet on stage, as SHE writes everything he says. When Paul was here there was no 'Praying and Worshiping' of anything. SHE started all this for HER Reptilian God, Kalaum! Oh yes! This does sound like Science Friction, but just like the ChemTrails in the sky, Fluoridated Water, GMO TechFood, Lethal Vaccines, HAARP, Microwave Cell Towers, Pharmaceuticals, and so much more that the public is dealing with, it is all a Bad Dream created to Kontrol & Kill people. TapLining is a Big Business today!

The 'Worshiping and Praying' to anything has been known throughout Human History and was originally started by Kults who did sacrifices, as Paul wrote about in his book, 'The Tigers Fang' in the chapter called, 'The Worship of Moloch.' Paul was very aware of the Reptilian Influence on the earth, but he did not want to get side tracked, as he was setting up the foundation for something so much bigger than just people looking to the same 'Old Gods' they have for eons. Paul started off with the 'God Idea' and Darwin and Harold were supposed to have expanded upon what Paul did, but they did not 'Listen' to The RealGuidance, and soon became their own 'Stars' for the onlooking members. From the year 1970, I was with what is Now known as the Krone Kontrolling Korporation (KKK) until August 3, 2001, when Paul, Rebazar and The Real UNUversal Guides gave me what was then The Rod of Power. At that time I was shown 'THE IS' The TruReality LifeIS. I was asked to expand upon what Paul had presented, and as of August 3, 2007, The Original Rod of Power was transformed into 'THE NUWAVIS THE NUMAN.' Most of the TapLined and Dumbed Down MemberShrimps under Reptilian Joanny and Puppet Master HarOld have not been paying attention to their DreamVisions, as many of them were not ready to Recognize THE ALLIS. The time has come for The NUNowniss of THE ALLIS. Most of this world is still 'seduced' with the 'god idea' and praying and worshiping to what most people know nothing about accept a 'mental idea' of Space Gods somewhere. People have been seduced to pour out their Emotional Love and become 'emotionally attached' to something they know nothing about, and while they are doing this, they are setup to be TapLined in their dreams by the Korporation Kontrollers of this world.

Just like in the movie, 'The Matrix' where Neo escapes his TapLines with the help of Morpheus, which is on YouTube as a segment called, 'Neo's Rebirth.' What is seen in 'The Matrix' is exactly what is taking place in today's world, but few people can 'See' this or relate to how it all works. Once YU, The RealU, has RealGuidance and a Real Education from Rebazar Tarzs & The RealGuides, YU will gradually start to See what I am Sharing here. YU must first start off with 'The NU-U Sessions' and have The RealConnection to The SoundLight Reality of THE ALLIS. What I am Sharing is not about any 'Belief' as the masses have been fed with this Reptilian Idea, because there is no such thing as 'Belief' of any form. LifeIS Real and moreso than the Creation we are in with our Five Psychic Bodies in time and space. YU have been mislead for lifetimes about what is taking place here and YU are still being mislead even though YU may 'Think' YU know what is going on here and also with any Political, Religious or Spiritual Idea YU have come to know or accept as your reality. Of course it is almost for certain YU will find what I am Sharing to be very interesting and at the same time YU will be very reluctant, because there are very few Real RiskTakers in Life. This NUBook is a 'Glimpse' as to what I have written over the years and with Sharing My RealExperiences. When YU learn to get beyond Your Literal Mind and all YU have come to know from the misinformation YU have been fed, YU will See what very few people ever do. Have Fun with this and Watch Your Dreams!

"AND HERE IS THE LATEST CROCK NEWS..."

From wherever we came from to Now, here we are with what seems to be something we all really need to know... **"The 6 O'Crock News!"** What has been created from 'Nothing' has all of a sudden become something that many people want to know about. Hello, I am Duane The Great Writer, and I am here to 'Simply Report The RealNews' and have fun with this idea. I LUV The RealAdventure in discovering 'What Has RealValue!' I already understand there are those on the earth who are only interested in themselves and what they can get, and also what they can get from others to the point of over-manipulation and Abusive Kontrol. This becomes their choice, and at the same time I am Living My Adventure and Reporting The RealNews how I See IT.

I have learned to make Better Choices for myself, while there are those who would rather deceive others and create things to 'Look Good' on the surface as their 'Business Fronts' with their Kontrolling Korporations' while they have their Secret Agendas to manipulate almost everything for themselves. I like Clean Air, Clean Water and anything that IS Real and Wonderful. There will always be those who like to distort and destroy what is already Natural & Beneficial, as we can easily See in the world around us. There is no mistake as to what is happening on the earth with all the pollution and poisoning, as it is purposely done every moment of everyday. And so what we see on television with what I refer to as 'The 6 O'Crock News' is just that, as it is mainly a Marketing Ploy for unaware people to 'Agree' to a Planned Distortion that Looks Good. YU have the right to decide whatever YU will. YU can just keep going along with what others decide for YU, or YU can WakeUp and be a part of creatively creating a RealBenefit for YourSelf and this world. For MySelf, I like to Take The Risk and create My Own Adventures and Doing Something Wonderful and Real. Not everyone will do this, because they are not ready to face themselves and what they have created in the past and what is Now right in front of them, so they would rather 'Pretend' that everything will be fine and that their Personal Life will be fine also. When YU learn to 'Read Between The Lines' as to what is being presenting and said from the

Political and Religious Kontrollers, YU will See that what they are doing is in no way a RealBenefit, accept for themselves to have More Kontrol and Obedience from those they look down upon, which is YU and others like YU. 'Pretty Words' do not make a person, nor how they dress and act and what they may give in public and to others. So much of the time their 'giving' is nothing more than a ploy for what they want and what they will get, which is usually everything others already own and have worked hard for. It is The RealHeart of a person that IS Real, that is if they have developed their RealHeart or simply educated themselves to the 'Standards' here where they have become rather cleaver at manipulating situations and people to their personal advantage. YU will always be the decider of Your Destiny.

A little over 200 years ago, what we are Now experiencing with all the Purposely Planned Pollution and Poisoning of just about everything in our lives did not exist at all. Poisoning has become a 'Standard' to be okay and acceptable. The Original American Indians did not do anything like what has swept across this world. YU can 'Believe' what YU see on TV with all the 'Sound-Good' reporting or YU can learn to investigate what is really taking place on the earth YU are part of. YU will be right back here in a much worse situation than what exists Now in future lifetimes if YU do not WakeUp to The Reality of Cause and Effect and how everything has its own outcome. The masses have been taught to 'Believe' in something and to use the ideas of good and bad to explain what is taking place with all the Causes and Effects we each experience. Only YU can decide if YU want to stay asleep to What LifeIS, The Whole of Life, or decide to have RealGuidance and a RealEducation to where YU will experience for YourSelf how to get all your own answers without the 'Officialness' of those who really do not know. There is no mistake as to what is taking place Here & Now. What I have written in this NUBook is a brief summary as to what has and is taking place. Of course, very few will agree with what I am presenting, which is fine, because not everyone is ready at this time to WakeUp and Become MoreAware. I suggest YU start to pay close attention to what is taking place with Your Life Now, because YU are all YU have. The challenge here is to survive and to continue to do so.

IN THEE BEGINNING THERE WAS...

... what the Originators of the Holey Dribble decided there would be, and so we will now take a trip back in time and experience some of what really happened when the Kalaum Grog's Reptilian Agents came to the planet earth and created the first two Humanoids... AKA...

ADUMB *and* EDAH

(AAA-DUMB / EEE-DAH)

IN THE BEGINNING... Grog decided to create the earth. HE had created a lot of other RoundWorlds, like Mars and Venus, but he was not happy how they came out. HE was really testing his imagination as to what to do. HE really wanted something different than the same old 'rock looking' planets with a lot of gray and dullness. HE imagined real hard and decided to try a new approach. HE thought that if he added some 'green' to the landscape it might help liven things up a bit. And so HE did his 'Hookus Pookus' (which is still very popular today) and suddenly HE had a giant glob of rock that was forming at an alarming rate. HE was getting very excited as to how it would turn out. After millions of earth years, which were merely seconds to Grog, the earth was looking really good. HE created a funny looking body for himself and appeared on the earths surface. As HE looked around HE was very pleased with HIMSELF, but there was this weird strange feeling within HIM that there was something missing. He walked around and around for the longest time, I would say about fifty million earth years or so, and then suddenly it struck HIM, just like one of HIS lightening bolts! "Aliens! I do need some Aliens on the earth to get things going!" HE thought out loud as lightening bolts shot in the sky.

Grog had his own strange sense of humor, but HE did give a 100% when it came to creating something. So, from the sky came hundreds of Reptilian Alien Spacecraft. Grog was very pleased, because it only took his Alien Buddies a few seconds to respond to Grog's texting of HIS thoughts to them. All around the Divine Grog the Spaceships landed. As the Reptilian Aliens exited their ships they paid great homage to their Lord and Master Grog of the Heavenly Worlds. As all the Aliens surrounded Lord Grog, they fell to their knees and put their faces to the dirt and yelled... "Oh Magical Grog, you are all there can ever be! We are here to serve and worship you! Tell us what you want and we will obey!" Said thousands of obedient Aliens all at once as they kept their lizard heads to the dirt. Grog looked around at his obedient worshipers. HE loved being worship and praised, because HE is a jealous Grog and there shall be no others but HIM to be worshiped and loved. Then HE said in a very demanding manner...

"Who amongst you will sacrifice themselves to ME, Your Grog?"

There was a very long silence, very long actually. After I do not how long, but it was really a long time, maybe a few thousand years, Grog became a bit beside HIMSELF and very demanding...

"WELL!?! Who will show ME their loyalty and sacrifice themselves for ME, Your Grog? Speak up or I will get rid of all of you!" HE said.

Again, there was a long silence, as Grog interrupted the silence and screamed out... "YOU IDIOTS!!!" And, at that very moment huge lightening bolts shot across the sky and came to earth and hit several hundred of the worshiping Aliens and they were instantly gone.

"HA, HA, HA, HA, HA, YOU FOOLS!!! YOU CANNOT MESS WITH THE POWERFUL AND LITERALLY KNOWING GROG!!! Get up you fools, I have a mission for you! You are to create Humanoids on the earth as your slaves and then build temples to ME, Your Grog."

The Aliens quickly pulled their faces from the ground and ran into their spaceships and in no time brought out a bunch of tools and materials and started building a structure to create the Humanoids. Everyone was very busy and Grog was very pleased. The Aliens were very fast, as they had built many structures on other planets for Grog. When the structure was completed, Grog walked inside, as there were a lot of Alien Doctors (like the ones on earth today) ready to perform what Grog wanted. As Grog looked at the Alien Doctors, HE gave them a command. They immediately went to work, and I would say in about a week or so they had completed creating the first two Humanoids.

"Excellent! Excellent!" Said Grog, as was so pleased with HIMSELF.

"I shall call Adumb, as the male species, and Edah as the woman! These are my first children upon the earth and as humans create their own history they will always remember Adumb and Edah," said Grog.

To become alive on the earth, the Humanoids needed a Soul to take on the Humanoid Body. Of course Grog was already ready for this, as he had sacrificed hundreds of his Alien Buddies and at the same time had them captive in the Astral Prisons until he needed them. He then summoned the Black Angel of Death, who brought forward two Alien Souls to enter the Humanoid Bodies. The Alien Souls resisted and tried to escape, as Grog knew they would, and so HE found the drama of their resistance very amusing. But the struggle was useless, as they were instantly stuck in the Humanoid Bodies and soon became unaware how they got there. Grog ordered Adumb and Edah to stand up and kneel before him, and so they did just what he wanted.

"Oh my children, you will become fruitcakes and multiply! That is an order!" Said Grog firmly to them, as they nodded their heads okay.

Grog was so very pleased at how everything had worked out, that he only sacrificed a dozen of the Alien Doctors to a horrible death and left several to clean up the mess, as HE usually sacrifices everyone doing the operations, but this time he was 'Feel'n Rather Good!

This is a rough idea as to how things got started on the earth, which most people have no idea of. What has been 'officially documented' among the Social Orders in modern society is an ingenious Fairy Tale contrived by the Reptilian Aliens to keep unaware souls as slaves to the Reptilian Political and Religious Orders. Grog had ordered his

Alien Scribes to create the Holey Dribble and to convince all those from the original Adumb and Edah to 'Believe' in the Written Word.

As the Alien Doctors were cleaning up the awful blue-blooded mess, Adumb and Edah followed Grog outside where he had a talk with them. They were to have specific instructions as to what to do...

"Okay you two, I want you to listen closely. I have created a place for you, and it is right over there," HE said as HE pointed in the distance.

Adumb and Edah turned and saw a lovely garden with green grass for miles all around and beautiful flowers everywhere. What really stood out the most was a giant tree right in the middle of everything.

"This is your new home and from here you will figure out what to do with yourselves for Eternity. HA! HA!" HE roared, as he vanished.

Adumb and Edah looked at each other and shrugged their shoulders at the same time, then casually walked over to the giant tree. They were both very curious as to what this place was all about. As they looked around they liked what they saw and smiled at each other. It really was a very lovely place, and without any chemical fertilizers. They both had a certain instinct to themselves, and as they began to use a little of their imagination, Adumb suddenly spoke...

"Can you speak Edah?" Asked Adumb, as he was hoping she would.

It took her a moment and then she said, "Yes, yes I can!"

They were both so happy, as they jumped up and down and danced around the big tree! As time went on their life was almost perfect, accept when Grog would make it rain and mess Edah's hair up, as HE thought this was funny! Then one morning as they both awoke from some very strange dreams they had, Adumb said to Edah...

"Was that you snoring last light? I could hardly sleep at all!" He said.

She looked at Adumb abruptly and said, “I do not snore, you must be hearing things! Besides, what is snoring?”

Adumb knew he heard something during the night, and as he laid back down and looked up into the tree he suddenly saw something moving. He jumped up immediately with his eyes wide open and walked around the tree. Edah looked at him and said...

“Adumb, what are you doing silly boy? Have you been smoking the weeds again? Haven't I told you not to do that, you DooDoo Bird!!

“I have not been smoking anything! There is something in this tree! Look for yourself! I saw it moving,” he said rather alarmed to her.

At first, Edah was not interested in what Adumb was saying, because as their relationship had progressed over time, she had become a bit bored with him. At first their love-making was exciting, but he soon lost interest and she did not like his attitude, so she liked to sulk a lot.

“If there is something in the tree, Numb Nuts, why don't you climb up and see what it is, I am not at all interested,” she said rather huffy.

Adumb was a little nervous to find out what was in the tree, but at the same time he didn't like the snoring at night, so he began to slowly climb the side of the big tree. As he was climbing he continued to look around, as he was a bit nervous about something that might jump out at him. As he reached the first big branch, he sat for a moment and tried to see thru all the dense leaves. He listened very closely as to any sound he could hear, but there was none, only a very soft gentle breeze moving the leaves slowly about. As he was looking around, there was a hint of something coming to him, as he could feel there really was something hidden among all the shadowy leaves. Adumb was now experiencing a new sensation, that of a mysterious element he had never noticed before. He was very curious, as he proceeded higher up the huge trunk and branch by branch with a great curiosity. Then, he suddenly heard a strange voice speaking directly to him...

“Have you found anything yet, numbskull?” Said Edah laughing.

Adumb shook his head and rolled his eyes and thought about the last time they made love, as he heard the sound of Edah's voice. He was now developing an attitude about HER and he was imagining all this drama that would possibly take place, as he knew he would be with HER for a long time, actually far too long. What Grog had created for them was becoming more like a nightmare than what Adumb thought was their 'Garden of Edah!” Of course, SHE, had to name the place after herself! This was okay at first, but as time went on and SHE became more demanding, he knew he should have had the lawyer make the contract 'Joint Custody' for the both of them. But at the time Edah thought that 'Joint Custody' meant that Adumb could smoke all the weed he wanted to and SHE could do nothing about it, so SHE demanded full title for HERSELF, and so be it! Adumb pushed his thoughts aside and kept climbing upward. This tree was really big, really big! Suddenly, he could see something a ways above him, and at the same time he heard a movement. While Adumb was climbing, something dropped to the ground right beside Edah. SHE looked over and picked it up and liked what SHE saw, and at the same time SHE did not know what it was. Then, SHE looked up to see if SHE could see Adumb, but SHE couldn’t. As Adumb climbed, he heard a voice...

“Hello Adumb, I have been waiting for you to find ME,” said the voice.

Adumb was very startled, as he had always thought that Edah and him were the only ones on earth, not including the stupid lawyer. Here was another new experience for Adumb and he was very curious as to who this was in the tree with him, so he said rather casually...

“Who are you?” He asked with a great curiosity.

“I am someone you have always known and you will always know and you will always love ME,” said the voice in a slithering manner.

Adumb searched thru his experiences and what he had come to know since he was on earth, but nothing showed up, and so he asked...

"Why are you here?"

"To help you do what you need to do," said the voice slithering.

"Really? What is it I need to do?" Asked Adumb wondering.

"You need to see and know what you need to do," said the voice.

Adumb never finished high school, so he was not the great brain nor a Literal Person. So, he just thought nothing and remained silent.

Then the voice appeared to Adumb and he was shocked!

"What are you?" He asked all excited like he was going to jump down.

"Don't be alarmed, you and I and Edah will be around for a long time together. We will all be the best of friends, you will see," Snakey said.

Snakey began to tell Adumb many things he did not know. They were up in the big tree for the longest time, I would say about fifty or sixty years according to earth time, because Snakey had a lot to tell. Then one day Adumb returned to Edah and brought Snakey with him...

"Did you miss me, dear?" Asked Adumb to Edah.

"What, I didn't even realize you were gone that long. Who's your new friend?" Asked Edah, as she seductively look at Snakey.

"This is Snakey, he has been here all along and he told me a lot of interesting things about what we are to do. Would you like to hear some of what he told me?" Asked Adumb, as he was about to speak.

"Not really, I am more interested in what HE can do for me!" Said Edah, as HER eyes met Snakey's and it was like an instant romance.

"You are really a big and long Snakey aren't you!" Said Edah, as SHE looked him over and HE began to smile from fang to fang with tongue.

Suddenly, Adumb got the hint and said, "I will leave you two alone and jog to the Dead Sea for some exercise and be back in a month."

With their eyes fixed upon each other, Edah and Snakey began to 'Get it On' and have the thrill of their life. After they were finished and they laid together under the big tree, Snakey said to Edah...

"You are terrific Edah! I have never experienced anyone like you! I must have you as my Mate forever!" HE said to HER.

"I really like you too, Snakey, you are so big and round and you fit so well inside of me," SHE said with HER seductive voice.

"You know that Apple I dropped for you to give to Adumb, I want you to have it, because it will open your eyes to a lot more than he can see. I want you to always be with me and rule all the earth and the other RoundWorlds and the Psychic Planes in time and space," HE said.

"Oh, that sounds fun, but you are just Snakey, a snake! How are you planning on ruling everything?" SHE asked with a great passion.

"Ha, ha, ha, I am so much more than a snake, I am Lord Grog, Grog of all I know," as HE turned into a Giant Reptilian Lizard twice as big as HER. "I have been waiting to see how you and Adumb would do on the earth. I truly thought he would do so much better than he has, but he was disappointed me, but you are so alluring and seductive. I want you with me to 'Influence' everyone who is to adore and worship me forever. Will you do this?" HE asked with a big slithering smile.

"Oh, you are so much bigger now than I could have ever imagined! Of course I will be your Mate as The Influence," as SHE bit into the Apple and felt a strange sensation go thru HER that SHE loved. SHE was now hooked with a huge passion to posses everything SHE wanted.

And so the story goes, as Grog created the earth, along with Adumb and Edah. It did not take Grog seven days to created the earth, with HIS Hookus Pookus it only took HIM a matter of moments and the earth was all ready to go. Now that Edah knew the Bigger Plan of Grog and what HE wanted for eternity, SHE was once again very interested in Adumb and creating new body types to capture more unaware souls who were on the various Psychic Planes. When Adumb returned from his jog, SHE and Adumb went at it for more than forty years. They produced thousands of offspring, and from their offspring came thousands more until there were millions all over the earth. Grog, from his huge castle in the Mental Plane, looked down upon the earth and was very happy. There were now so many more worshipers that knew about Grog from what SHE and Adumb had created. Of course, there were those who did not agree to all the rules, regulations and restrictions SHE loved to created, so SHE would cleverly instigate a few wars here and there to drive fear into the hearts of those who did not worship and obey the commandments of Lord Grog. After many centuries had passed, Edah had done HER job so well on the earth and brought so many unaware souls to their knees, that when HER body was finally withered and worn out, Grog brought HER Core to HIS castle and SHE has been there ever since.

As My RealAdventures continues as Duane The Great Writer, I have written about The Influence in 'The AdventurIS Series.' To most of this world where pollution and being poisoned is a way of life, most people cannot See what is happening right in front of them and how The Influence Kontrols almost everyone and everything. The governments of this world, the Korporations, the Belief Systems, all are Kontrolled by SHE, The Influence. The Authoritarians, who are subject to Cause and Effect from the Lords of Karma, are the slaves to Lord Grog, as they 'Think' they are the ones with the Power and Kontrol over others, as this is all a Marketing Ploy by the Kalaum Grog to deceive all those HE can and to have them worship and pray to HIM. Grog is the King Kult Kon of the Psychic Planes and almost everyone likes to Blindly Worship HIM. Stay tuned for more RealAdventures with Duane and The RealGuides, as there is a lot more to learn in time and space!

ONCE UPON A TIME IN TIME AND SPACE ...

... along came Mr. Paul. Mr. Paul was not your average person, he could See things that others could not. He had been trained by the best and was going to put what he had learned to the test. He decided to have his own business, and he decided that it would be a rather 'spirited' business, not just something ordinary like so many other businesses and easy to understand, but something exceptional. Mr. Paul started off by writing articles in newspapers and magazines, and then he went out into the public and began to lecture to people. At first there were very few who were interested, but as time went on and he kept at it, there were soon thousands who were paying for his writings and going to his seminars. After a few years life was good and Mr. Paul was doing very well as he toured around the country and met a lot of people that liked what he had to say. Mr. Paul had given himself the title of 'The Living Master' which a lot of people liked. As the years went by people from all over the world knew Mr. Paul, even diplomats and dignitaries. But, like all good intentions, and Mr. Paul's was very good and honorable, someone decided to get rid of him. And so in 1971, Mr. Paul was no longer here, but the Business Corporation he started was still here. His wife took possession of the business and handed it over to a fellow named Mr. Darwin. There was some kind of a deal made, but nobody really knows what it was.

Enter the new Living Master, as this is what Mr. Darwin decided to call himself as did Mr. Paul. Mr. Darwin was now the head of a large organization and began to do business as usual. All the paying members were a bit shocked by Mr. Paul's passing and a lot of them left, but there were still thousands all over the world who were going to stick it out with the new Living Master. As time went on, the business which Mr. Paul originally called 'SEEK' was now doing better than ever, and Mr. Darwin was very happy with all the money and attention. So happy indeed, that he took a lot of the profits and secretly built himself a nice big house in another state. But for Mr. Darwin, who was now The Living Master and like a big movie star with the paying members, he figured he could have whatever he wanted, including any woman he wanted, and he had many. This is all fine, as it was his business and the paying members wanted Mr. Darwin to be happy and to keep telling them his 'Pretty Words' at the seminars. He was happy, the paying members were happy, this really does seem like a happy story, but as we go along here it gets even more interesting.

Mr. Darwin had many employees that he paid a very minimum wage to, very minimum, because he really needed the millions that he was raking in moreso than those who were barely paying their rent in the cheapest places they could find. To Mr. Darwin, what he was doing made perfect sense, that is until one of the employees, a Mr. Harold, found out what Mr. Darwin was doing. Mr. Harold informed the Bored Directors, and so a big meeting was held and it was decided that Mr. Darwin was to step back and let Mr. Harold be The Living Master. This does sound like an easy transition, but there were law suits and a lot of tugging and pushing until finally Mr. Darwin gave in. Mr. Darwin hung around a while, as Mr. Harold was sympathetic, because Mr. Darwin did build the corporation a lot bigger. At first, the acceptance of Mr. Harold was not good at all, but finally he had made his place in the corporation and things began to get back to 'business as usual.' Mr. Harold was a rather reserved fellow, as he had very humble beginnings. He was a married man and had a young daughter. As time went on, Mr. Harold began to see past what he had always known, because he was The Living Master and his title was a big deal to the paying membership, as they loved paying their Living Master.

It wasn't too long until SHE showed up! SHE had only one intense purpose to do one specific thing and one thing only... to takeover what Mr. Harold had acquired. I ask you, does this sound like Science Friction or what? On this earth this scenario happens all the time, but to The Living Master? NO! It cannot in any way happen to the so-called spirited man that is so loved by the paying members! That would be ridiculous! What is SHE thinking and trying to do? Who would 'believe' such a thing could happen to someone such as The Living Master who seems to know all there is about Life. Well, it did happen and far beyond what anyone could even imagine. I am glad this story is just Science Friction, because who would 'believe' any of this to be possible? As time went on, SHE became more and more directed to Her goal, as SHE got Mr. Harold to divorce his wife and SHE stepped in to more than take her place. Now SHE could see an even cleared picture of what SHE was to do with her new husband that was becoming like putty in HER hands. SHE way very excited as they were now man and wife, as HER whole intent was on using Mr. Harold to get what SHE wanted for those SHE was secretly working for. The Friction here gets better all the time! SHE was working very hard at the corporation, and it really did 'look' like SHE was doing a great job. SHE was so willing to edit what Mr. Harold wrote and to even make suggestions as to what to say when he was on stage looking down upon all the paying members, so SHE gave him notes.

AHHHHHH, life was now so good for HER! She was taking total Kontrol! The Bored Directors had become very Dumbed Down by Her, and so whatever SHE wanted SHE got. The Korporation was now taking on a very defined direction and SHE was in charge, but of course to make things 'look good' SHE made it look like Mr. HarOld, The Living Master was in charge. SHE was very cleaver as SHE got almost everyone to agree to whatever SHE did. When Mr. Paul created his corporation, it was for the sole purpose of showing people how to Become MoreAware, but this was not HER intention at all! SHE wanted absolute Kontrol, because SHE was sent to keep the members from Becoming MoreAware and to be Kontrolled by HER. SHE had now become, 'Krone, The Influence of the Three Headed Grog,' as SHE had earned HER title according to the Kalaum Grog, SHE was secretly working for. Krone is a multidimensional Reptilian Alien! SHE was sent to earth to takeover the SEEK Corporation, because it was interfering with all the other Kontrolling Reptilian Kalaum Businesses on the earth. The members had become aware of so many things, including other dimensions and the Kalaum Grog Himself. Kalaum Grog did not like this, so he sent His Mistress, The Influence, to take over the body and mind of Mr. HarOld's wife Joanny. I know exactly what YOU are thinking! How could this possible be? The Living Master who is so admired and loved, plus he has a huge paying membership, and best of all he had built a beautiful temple for people to adore him in. What could possibly be better than this with all he had worked so hard for? Anything can happen with Science Friction and it sure did with Mr. Harold. He was not aware at all at what Krone was doing, but as things became so very good for him, he really was not interested in what SHE was doing, as he was more interested in his own position as The Living Master. He could now do no wrong, as everything he was doing made perfect sense to him and he was very happy with the outcome, because he was rich and famous! What could be better than this, he thought to himself?

On the earth, everyone has the right to do any business they like, and especially if it is in the United States of America! In America, anyone can create whatever they want to, just like those who run and own The United States Korporation in Washington D.C. Honesty, integrity, truthfulness, these ideas and so many more can be part of any business, but there are always those who are not interested in being equal to others, but must do devious things to show they are better than others. It has become a way of life on the earth for many Kontrolling Korporations and many of the Governmental Systems to outright deceive others for the sole purpose of power, money and Kontrol. This is the idea of 'doing business' as usual. Krone was not going to reinvent the wheel, so to speak, SHE simply copied what every other Reptilian Kontroller was doing on earth, and by doing so, SHE became very successful. The hard working supporting people of the earth have been so Dumbed Down and Marketed with Deception, most of them cannot see thru what is always right in front of them.

With all this and a whole lot more going on, Now comes The Fun Part! Enter, Duane The Great Writer, as I am the one who is writing this and I also have lived this Science Friction Adventure! Of course, very few if any will 'believe' me, as I do have a very creative imagination. Does it make a bit of sense that any of this really took place and is still going on today? Of course not! I just like to write about things that are Fun! And so, let's get on with the rest of the story... A funny thing happened in 2001, and that is, I was asked by some Very Special Beings to handle a Really Big Assignment. I immediately jumped at the chance and said "YES!" 2001, became a turning point in America and the world, as 911 occurred right after I was given My Assignment. The world was Now a different place, as was when we entered the Atomic Age. In My Dimensional Dreams, I was shown what most people have no idea even exists. The Special Beings had shown me what had taken place with Mr. Darwin and also Mr. HarOld and his Reptilian Mate Krone. I was now into 'An Adventure Like No Other' and Luving IT! I had a family at the time and they thought I was just 'telling stories' about what I was experiencing, so I eventually left them and headed out on my own. It was not an easy time for me, but I could See what others could not and I kept my focus on What IS Real Now.

As the years went by I kept writing My NUBooks and people would contact me and take My TruCourse. While I was doing all this, I was also Seeing Krone and her Witch Hearted Kronies, TapLining HER MemberShrimps in their Dimensional Dreams. SHE wanted Absolute Kontrol over their emotions and mind and SHE was getting HER way, as most of the Dumbed Down MemberShrimps were more than willing to be subjected to Alien Injections in their Unseen Astral Bodies. The Living Master HarOld was now completely TapLined by HER and very agreeable to everything SHE was doing. He has a great life thanks to HER and all HER Kontrol. In 2001, when I was given My Assignment to continue with what Mr. Paul had originally started, there were a lot more changes in Life than what has taken place on the earth. The Whole of Life had decided to provide a NUWay for people to Become MoreAware than what Mr. Paul had started. I was to let this world know about what Krone was doing and also what the OneWorld Kontrollers had been doing to people for thousands of years. I was paying close attention to My Dimensional Dreams and what I was being shown and guided to do. At the same time I met other Seers who would help me, as they also saw what the Dumbed Down Goofus Living Master was doing with his Alien Mate. Today, because of all the TapLining in the world, many people are sick, ill and have so many varieties of cancers, and of course it is all like 'hookus pookus' when it comes to discovering what is really taking place, as most people 'believe' the Mad Scientists that have created an 'Officialness of

Nonsense' for the masses to gladly accept as something genuine. A whole other world of strangeness has Now emerged since Mr. Paul was here. I am in the very center of all that is taking place with those who are Waking Up and Becoming MoreAware. I have contacts with so many people, but most of them are so fearful of the Kontrolling Korporations and those who use Alien TapLines in their Dimensional Dreams. Fortunately, what I am Sharing here is just Science Friction and nothing to be concerned about from all the 'Agreement' that is taking place with what most people have no idea is really happening.

It seems to be so much better for people to be very unaware and oblivious to what is really Kontrolling and harming them, and so with all the 'Pretty Words' from Politicians and Religious Kontrollers, it seems to make more sense to most people to stay Dumbed Down and continue into more unconscious lifetimes as they have come from in the past. This is the right of every person to do so, and I for one would not try to convince anyone otherwise. I would say that what the Existing Invented Systems, along with The TapLining Living Master HarOld and his Reptilian Mate Krone have done has been nothing less than remarkable. They have worked very hard to make sure as few people as possible know what they have been secretly doing and are still doing on a grand scale today. But I must confess, in Creation there is always Cause and Effect, whether people 'believe' this or not, and so everything will show up no matter how well it is hidden and disguised. Master HarOld and his Alien Joanny have accumulated huge amounts of Karmic Debt with all they are doing, but what does this matter in a world where most people are so Literalized into 'Thinking' they already know everything they need to know? To the Scholastically Educated, what they have come to know with their Printed Degrees is that they know more than Life ITSelf. People are living in a Science Friction World, and when they read a story such as this, it is all Science Friction and how could it possibly be anything at all. Each of us decides what we want to be real and no one can convince us otherwise until we have our own experiences that prove differently. There will always be more to My RealAdventures to See and Become MoreAware. YU have this opportunity Now... Have Fun!

KRONE TAPLINING INKORPORATED

"DUANE THE GREAT NOTHING!!!" Yelled Baloney Joanny, as SHE pointed HER squirt gun at the computer screen. "I am sick of 'Duane The Great Writer' and all his Stupid Jokes, Pictures and Books of me!"

Then the phone rings and the secretary answers, "Hello, TapLining InKorporated, may I help you?" A question is asked and she replies, "No Sir, we do not have any information on TapLining your mother, but if you look on the Internet you may find something." The caller thanks her as she says, "Your welcome and 'May The Burdens Be!"

"Who was that, Bubbles?" Asked BJ in a sarcastic voice.

"Someone who wanted information on how to TapLine their mother," said Bubbles, as she politely replied to BJ.

"That's a good idea, we should make some brochures on TapLining everyone! Where's Harry?" Asked BJ in a demanding voice.

"I saw him go into the bathroom yesterday and I haven't seen him since," said Bubbles, as she knew BJ would not like this.

Baloney Joanny immediately got up and walked over to the bathroom door and started beating on it... "Are you in there Harry?!! Are you watching Kartoons again and being stupid at the same time?" SHE roared as there was a silence for the longest time. "Bubbles, did you remove the TV from the bathroom like I asked you to do?"

"Yes Miss Joanny, I did exactly like you asked," said Bubbles.

"Well, then what is he doing in there?" SHE asked very sternly, as SHE banged on the door and yelled again at Harry in the bathroom.

As SHE listened, Joanny could hear a very low voice mumbling thru the door to HER. "Is that you Harry? Speak up! What are you doing in there?" SHE again asked as Harry's voice became a little louder...

"I caught my tie on the toilet lever and I have been tied up here," he said with a very shy and embarrassed voice.

"What?! Are you stupid or what?!! You have been in there since yesterday and 'Now You Are Telling Me This!!!!!' "Bubbles, I want you to break down the door and get him out of there, he has to get ready to say his 'Pretty Words' to the MemberShrimps at the seminar!"

"I don't know if I can do that Miss Joanny, I am not very strong and that is a thick door," said Bubbles, as she really did not want to do it.

"Don't just sit there! What do I pay you for?" Said Joanny on fire.

"Ahhh... Miss Joanny, you don't really pay me, I have been recruited and intimidated with the idea that I am doing a Spiritual Service for you and Master Harry, and I would do anything, but I cannot break down the bathroom door for you," she said a bit nervous.

"Okay, okay, I will do it," as Joanny stepped back from the door to the other side of the room and prepared HERSELF to run to the door and bust it down, and as SHE ran forward, and at the very moment SHE got to the door at full speed, Harry opened the door and said...

"LOOK! I got my tie untied," as Joanny plowed into him and they both landed in the toilet. Bubbles was so shocked she began to laugh and laugh and could not stop laughing. Joanny and Harry were stuck together with their arms wedged into the toilet seat. "Stop that laughing Bubbles and help us get out of here!!!" Said Baloney Joanny.

"Oh Miss Joanny, with all the years I have worked here and given my services to you and Old Master Harry, I have to say that I have had enough! You can figure out your own life now... Have Fun!" She said. And so for now we will leave Phoney Baloney Joanny and Old Master Harry to their fate, which many more are Waking Up to Right Now!!!

ASK EVA NOW ABOUT PAUL TWITCHELL

Eva Shari, Eva SharIS, is having RealExperiences with Paul Twitchell and Rebazar Tarzs. Rebazar Tarzs taught Paul & Duane to provide a NUPresentation for Everyone. It has been a Huge Challenge to bring forth THE NUWISDOM OF THE ALLIS. There are so many who want to stay Restricted and Dumbed Down by the Kontrolling Korporations and their TapLining Masters. LifeIS ITSelf, and Free Will is the reality we each experience as we are all in Life and decide what our position will be. Everyone is 'Right' with the choices they are making, but for those who have The RealCourage to SeeMore than they ever have before, they will Become Aware of the fact that just being 'Right' is not enough. LifeIS a RealPurpose... This IS Real Now! To have a personal life to just survive on the earth and the other RoundWorlds is a step we must each go through until we have the opportunity to Wake Up to the Endlessniss LifeIS. Because the Kontrolling Korporations have deceived most people, it is a struggle to SeeThru what has been created that 'Looks So Good' and officially authentic, but is nothing more than Deceptive Marketing Ploy to keep YU here for Lifetimes.

Paul Twitchell brought forth what few people will ever understand during this lifetime, and what he presented has nothing to do with what the TapLining Master HarOld and his Reptilian Wife Joanny are doing Now. This world and many others like it are under Absolute Kontrol and it will always be so. The Political and Religious Systems use every Tactic and Marketing Ploy to Kontrol people's minds and emotions. The Biggest Ploy of all is the 'God' idea that was originally created by the Reptilian Aliens who first came to this planet and who have the majority of Kontrol on earth today. When Paul was here he gave a brief description of what was really taking place, and because this world has become a lot worse, it is Now my task to 'Report The News' as to what is happening Now, otherwise the masses will be worshipers and slaves of the Authoritarians and their Invented God for many more lifetimes to come. All of this is a 'Choice' as to The Real Awareniss of each person. A lifetime is but a 'wisp' in the wind and one's attention can go anywhere. THE NUWAVIS THE NUMAN NOW!

ASK EVA ABOUT THE NUWAVIS THE NUSOUND

Eva has had lifetimes of experience to where she Now Recognizes The NUSound of The TruReality LifeIS and what ALLIS The Natural Environment that Supports ALL of US. Thru the many ages of Human History there have been various 'Sounds of Life' that have been Shared. All sounds have their place like that of the ocean, the wind, waterfalls, sound of rain and that of all the Natural Sounds of Nature. Eva has Become Aware of these sounds and also The NUSound with ALLIS The Natural Environment, The NU-U. In Creation there are many sounds, but it is from a very special source that The NU-U IS from. As a person Tests The NU-U Sessions, they will begin to discover NUWorlds & Real UNUverses that have been unknown to them. The Sounds of Life are all around us and at the same time with us, but it is up to each of us to discover them or not. Like many of us, Eva has decided to explore what very few people ever will. What has been created on the earth takes the attention of most people and they are unaware of what else is possible accept as a temporary life here.

Eva IS Sharing Something Wonderful from The Natural Environment that is a RealBenefit for Everyone. Even though so much of what people are experiencing on the earth as an education and business seems to be the only way of life there is, there is also a lot more that is hidden and unseen by most. Duane The Great Writer is providing The NUPresentation as a WorldWide WakeUp Call for The ALLNatural Environment that Supports ALL of US. THE NUWAVIS The NUSound LifeIS, and this can be tested by anyone. Not everyone is ready to Become MoreAware at this time, as this entails a Huge Adventure like no other. The Whole of LifeIS about Becoming MoreAware, and as this is Recognized and Seen from more than just the Personal Senses and an Educated Mind, each person discovers for themselves they have so many more possibilities than they can even imagine. We will each be here for such a short time, then move into another unknown position that many are not ready for. The NU-U Sessions provide an avenue to See Beyond this world and into what else is possible for each person to discover for themselves. This adventure never ends!

YU CAN ASK EVA NOW ABOUT EVA

Everyone wants to know 'About Eva' and what she is doing with THE NUWAVIS THE NUMAN and The ALLNatural Environment. Eva has went thru a lot to come into The NUNowniss of THE ALLIS with Rebazar Tarzs & The RealGuides, and Now Eva is Sharing her Real Experiences with those who are ready to WakeUp and Become More Aware. Eva was once with the Kontrolling Kult Korporation of Krone, the Kalaum God and her TapLining Master, but Now, Eva IS Awake & Aware of the Marketing Ploy and Deception of Politics, Religion and so many Spiritual Paths with their worshiping to Invented Gods. Eva has Become MoreAware and can Now 'Recognize' she does not need a membership, initiations, guidelines, TapLining Masters, Kontrolling Reptilians and their Korporation 'Fronts!' Eva has taken the time to Test The NU-U Sessions and made The RealConnection with Rebazar Tarzs & Paul Twitchell. Eva has RealGuidance with The TruReality LifeIS, THE ALLIS. Eva watches her DreamVisions and IS Wonderful.

Eva IS Sharing a 'WorldWide WakeUp Call' with The NUPresentation Foundation, a California ALLHumanitarian Community Organization. What Eva IS Sharing entails The NUBooks of Duane The Great Writer and The ALLSolar Research Vessel Project for The Children of The World. Eva knows there is a lot more taking place on the earth Right Now than most people are aware of, and so Eva has decided to BE a Real RiskTaker and take on The Huge Challenge of Sharing Something Wonderful and Real with Everyone. Eva can See that most people like to 'Agree' to all the 'Restrictions' that have been invented and marketed to people to where they 'Think' they are free in some way, but actually the opposite is true once they pay attention to their DreamVisions. Life will show each person how they have 'Agreed' to a Purposely Planned Poisoning of this planet and are being used as slaves to support the Kalaum Korporations of the Social Systems. YU can learn to 'WakeUp Now' if YU have the courage to do so, or stay as YU are and obey all the Restrictions the Kontrolling Korporations want YU for. Eva IS Sharing what RealFreedom IS, apart from those who only 'imply' some sort of freedom. It is up to YU to decide. Have Fun!

KULT KORPORATIONS KONTROL THE EARTH

Everything here is based upon 'Agreement!' This is Very Real and not totally understood accept by those who Kontrol almost everything. YU do have a choice, but YU also need The RealKnowledge of THE IS to See Thru all the Purposely Planned Deception YU are living in Now. It has all become a 'Standard' for YU to Agree to whatever is 'Officially' created with the rules, regulations, doctrines and laws from those who really do not have any concern for The RealU, Your RealAwareniss. YU have to decide to Become MoreAware or stay Dumbed Down and Kontrolled for more unconscious lifetimes of the same drudgery and poisoning that is taking place Right Now. It is the Kalaum God Kults that rule the earth and all the RoundWorlds in time and space. YU have been forced to 'Believe' and worship the Invented Gods from the Original Reptilians who first came here and created the Humanoids.

To worship or pray to anything is a form of Kult, whether those who own the Earthly Korporation (EK) are being nice or not, they are being Kontrolled and TapLined by the Kalaum Governor God, Ruler over the Four PsycRealms and the Authoritarians who are his Political Puppets on all the Solid RoundWorlds. YU have been here thousands of lifetimes doing exactly what YU are doing Now, Agreeing to all the Purposely Created Restrictions to keep YU a little slave and prisoner and subject to your mind and emotions. YU may 'Think' YU have free will and a choice as to what your life is, but this is not so, and as YU creatively 'Sing The NU-U Sessions' and Watch Your DreamVisions, YU will be shown a whole NULife that is yours if YU will Take The Risk and do Something Wonderful for The RealU, Your RealAwareniss.

LifeIS what YU make it, and as YU can easily See, this planet is being poisoned every moment of every day and very little is being done about it. There is no mistake as to what is taking place here, but YU do have a chance to do so much better. YU are a 'Free Being of RealLight' but YU must decide to WakeUp and 'Recognize' this for YourSelf, because the Kontrolling Korporations are not going to do anything for YU accept keep YU a Prisoner here! Have Fun Deciding!

ASK EVA & DUANE NOW ABOUT YOUR NUJOURNEY

This world as we know it has been subjected to, and for the longest time, a One-Dimensional Kontrol. May individuals are Waking Up to What LifeIS Now, but there will always be those who want to hang onto the 'idea' that they must Kontrol others to have some kind of life here. The masses have been educated and taught they 'need' all kinds of 'Restrictions' with their lives to live here, as if this 'Place in Space' s not hard enough. From the Political, Religious, Spiritual, and Educational Systems of Kontrol, we are all subject to regulations and rules that bury a person with so many psychological symptoms that are not necessary at all. Eva & Duane are here to Share Something Wonderful & Real with Everyone. The Whole of Life really does make sense, and as each of us explore and experience whatever we do, we eventually begin to Recognize how to Become MoreAware and to finally free ourselves from what others have decided is all for them.

YU are a Free Being of Light, and with what DUANE THE GREAT WRITER is presenting as RealGuidance and a RealEducation, YU will be able to experience what most people know nothing about. The so-called 'official' Systems of the Earthly Korporations have fooled people into 'Thinking' they must 'Agree' to Kontrolling Restrictions to have a life here and survive, but this is not so. There is always a better and NUWay to See and Live and to BE Wonderful. This is Real Now, and what we are doing is so much More Fun than just an 'idea' like all the Belief Systems that have been invented to burden people. I am Simply Reporting The News and Living My Adventure and doing My Part to Share Something Wonderful with this world. Miss Eva is with me on this Journey to RealFreedom as she LUVs to Share with ALL.

YU Now have a Real Opportunity like never before to Become More Aware and Wonderful for YourSelf. Like the Sun Shining in the Sky, YU are a Free Being of Light and we will show YU how to Recognize YourSelf, The RealU, and Recognize The RealFreedom YU have been searching for as YU have went thru many lifetimes to come into The NUNowniss of The TruReality LifeIS, THE ALLIS. We Are Fun!

REBAZAR TARZS & PAUL TWITCHELL SING THE NU-U

When Paul Twitchell created his Corporation for this world, he also brought forth what he called the Charged Word of HU. When I was first a member of Paul's Corporation, the HU Word did work and make a connection to the Light and Sound, Paul referred to. When Paul left this life and Darwin Gross came to be the next master, he was given the duty of taking care of Paul's creation and to continue with what The Real UNUversal Guides wanted for the people of earth. Darwin started off okay, but at a certain point he became more interested in himself and what he could get from the membership. So, The Real Guides brought in Harold Klemp. Harold took over and he was fine until SHE arrived and totally subdued him to his knees to the Kalaum God! This would seem like a Good Fairy Tale, but it is not! HarOld is Now so TapLined from HER and buried in the Lower Astral Worlds with his Reptilian Mate Joanny, that it is almost doubtful he will ever get out of the PsycRealms. SHE came to take over and SHE has!!!

When I, Duane The Great Writer, was given The Real Rod of Power in 2001 from Rebazar & Paul, I was shown that the HU Word was destroyed by THE IS, The TruReality LifeIS, IS THE ALLIS. Reptilian Joanny and her Kontrolling Krone Korporation has convinced the Dumbed Down MemberShrimps that they must worship and pray to the Kalaum God and be a part of the Sacrificial Religious Priests that the Kalaum God supports with the RoundWorlds in time and Space. SHE has totally possessed HarOld, who is now the TapLining Master and has infected thousands upon thousands of unaware people with Reptilian TapLines in the unseen Astral Bodies of the membershrimps. Rebazar Tarzs, Paul Twitchell & The RealGuides are telling everyone who will listen to ***"Sing The NU-U Now"*** to break the TapLines set by TapLining Master HarOld and his Reptilian Mate Joanny. The NU-U Session IS The RealConnection to THE ALLIS. In 2007, The Rod of Power became, THE NUWAVIS THE NUMAN NOW. For those who pay attention to The RealGuidance from Rebazar Tarzs, they will be shown in Your DreamVisions, What IS Real Now! THE ALLIS decides The NUSound and The RealConnection... IT IS The NU-U-U-U Now!!

EVA & DUANE LUV TO SHARE

THE NUWAVIS THE NUMAN, Duane The Great Writer. As I stand in The RealPosition with The RealGuides, I have asked Eva Shari to join me, as we both stand in THE NUWAVIS NOW. Many people are now having RealSide Experiences with us Being Together. This was all set into motion long ago for this very moment with The NUNowniss of THE IS. Miss Eva & I are here everyday for everyone. Those who sincerely test The NU-U Sessions will find us with Rebazar Tarzs & The RealGuides on The RealSide and in Your DreamVisions. There can only be one way to RealTruth & RealFreedom, and that is to Become MoreAware and Recognize THE ALLIS. The Gods of Man had their day and they will not be forgotten, as they are an excellent reference and comparison to What IS Real Now. This is the 'idea' of Creation, to have something to compare with The TruReality LifeIS, which in turn gives us a TruVU, so as to Recognize The Whole of Life.

We have all been here many times before, and not because of the Gods of Man, which most people 'believe' is the case, but from what we each have decided to experience here to Become MoreAware. It has been a brainwashing technique that a 'god' created us and we are subservient to this god and must endure all the intimidation and fear this god gives us, so that we can eventually go to this gods heaven, which most have no idea where this is or even the god himself is. All this and so much more that has been 'Created' here is nonsense and has nothing to do with The TruReality LifeIS, THE ALLIS. All of us have gone through so much for lifetimes, and mainly being slaves to the Invented Systems. I am not being disrespectful, but it is time to Get Real with what is really taking place on this planet Right Now.

Eva & I are Sharing Something Wonderful and The TruReality that YU are a Being of Light, and not just another worker moving around on this Dirt World. As YU read this NUBook, YU will gain a Huge Insight and begin to SeeMore than YU have ever seen before, and it is ALL About YU! YU no longer have to bow, worship and fear a Ghostly God that was invented by the DarkBrats who rule this planet... not at all!!!

YU ARE AGREEING TO KONTROLLING RESTRICTIONS

'Agreement' is what makes anything possible. This IS How LifeIS! YU (YU / The RealU / This is who I am referring to) are 'Agreeing' to Purposely Planned Restrictions and Kontrol. YU may 'Think' your life is fine, but as YU learn to SeeMore than YU ever have before, then YU will Become MoreAware of all the Restrictions and Kontrol YU are Now Agreeing to. It is not about 'good or bad' in the sense that YU have been taught here, it is all a matter of Your Choice. The Kontrolling Systems, that of Political, Educational, Religious, Belief, and all the rest that have created Rules and Regulations to live by, and especially those that get people to worship, pray and perform ceremonies and rituals, they have marketed the public into 'Agreeing' with what they have created as something far more than it is. Most people are 'chasing' happiness, and those who know how to Kontrol others create something that 'supposedly' makes people happy, and so people 'Think' they are experiencing happiness by what has been created in Creation. RealHappiness is not found in Creation, but with Your RealAwareniss and being able to 'Recognize What IS Real Now!'

The unaware masses have been taught to look to Human History, Tradition and Ritualizm as a way of life. People have been purposely and cleverly educated to obey Restrictions, so as to be Kontrolled and Manipulated as supporters for the Ruling Invented Systems. As I am Reporting The News, the idea here is not to rebel in any outward mannerism, but to moreso learn to Recognize The RealU. LifeIS ALL About Becoming MoreAware! This IS Real Now! The Kontrolling Systems have wrapped their Created Restrictions in nicely wrapped packaging to get YU to 'Agree' to Them. YU have been doing this for untold lifetimes, as they have kept YU asleep to their process They have put YU thru, but YU no longer have to 'Agree' unless YU want to keep going into a future where there is no future for YU, accept to Agree with Them and continually be Kontrolled. This IS really how The Whole of LifeIS, YU are always the Decider and what YU Decide Becomes So. The TruReality LifeIS, THE ALLIS, has ITS own NUWay with ITSelf, and this has always been so, but most of those in their Operating Embodiments (OE) are not paying attention to What LifeIS

Sharing all the time with each one here. Your DreamVisions is a way to See Beyond this world of Planned Restrictions. Instead of always 'Thinking' what YU know, try letting 'Life Show YU What IS Real Now!'

YU will be very surprised at what will be 'Demonstrated' to YU when YU Sincerely want to learn and SeeMore. Your biggest hurdle will always be YourSelf, as LifeIS Already Perfect and Everything IS Already in its right place, so to speak, so it is really up to YU what YU will do with Your Life Now. YU can always stay as YU are and keep 'Agreeing' to all the Purposely Planned Restrictions and all the ones that will be continually created to Restrict YU even more, or YU can Test what I am Presenting YU Now. The Whole of LifeIS ALL About Becoming MoreAware and Sharing The TruReality LifeIS we are each discovering that provides a RealBenefit For ALL. It is so that on this hard material world we do have businesses, and this is fine, but when 'doing business as usual' means YU sacrificing Your RealAwareniss to something Kontrolling and Temporary, YU always have the Choice to make a better decision, that is if YU have The RealCourage to do so. YU have been taught to 'Fear' the Kontrolling Systems that have been invented out of nothing from an 'idea' from a limited embodiment. This is Real Now! No matter what has been created here it has nothing to do with The Whole of Life, The TruReality LifeIS. Creation is not all there is to Life, it is only something that we each decide and then we 'Agree' to it. Test The NU-U Sessions and let Life show YU a lot more.

All the ideas of Rituals, Worship, Prayer, Initiations, Followers, Paths, Politics, Religion, Spiritual, Meditation, Gods, Saviors, Guidelines, Regulations, Commandments, Rules, Laws, Legal, Moral, Paganizm, Atheist, Rulers, Commanders, Presidents, Kings, Queens, and so much more, have all been Devised to Kontrol Everyone into a Blind Submission. ALLIS The Natural Environment! This IS Real Now! Where can YU find with The Natural Environment, that of the beautiful embodiments with the Birds of the Air, Dolphins and Fish of the Sea, Animals of the Land, that there are Self-imposed Restrictions? Only those who have an Earthly Body with Their Mind focused on creating something that does not exist with The Natural Environment have created all the Restrictions and Poisons that have polluted the entire planet, which is now heading for a demise. YU can 'Pretend' all YU want to with your present lifestyle here that things will get better, but those who are in Absolute Kontrol of the earth are not interested with what YU want or think. They, the DarkBrats, have their own Planned Agenda, which they have proven Over and Over again throughout Human History, and very few of those who have 'Agreed' to be subject to all Their Purposely Planned Invented Restrictions have taken the time to Recognize what has always been right in front of them. YU really do have a Choice, but it will take everything YU have to make it Real Now, or YU will once again be floating down the muddy river with all those who are still unaware of their RealAwareniss, and 'over the falls' once again and back down into the gloom of struggling for a bit of light to see past all the darkness. Life Really Does Make Sense, once YU know how to make sense of it, and IT IS ALL About Recognizing What IS Real Now. The past can be a good 'reference' but nothing that can be lived again, so 'dragging' it with YU will not do anything for YU, accept to keep YU in Old Drama and 'Hoping' for something. YU can Decide whatever YU want to Now. YU are creating Your Future!

The TruReality LifeIS, IS Always Now. LifeIS an ISNESS, just as the Sun in the Sky IS Always Shining, this is a RealExample of The Whole of Life, as ALLIS The Natural Environment that supports ALL of US. YU have been very cleverly taught with the Invented Systems that Restrictions are a 'way of life' here, and that it is best for YU to 'Agree' or 'things will happen' to YU that YU will not like. This and so much more have been Purposely Planned Fear Tactics to get YU to be a hard working supporter of those who do not want to do their share, but steal from YU what YU have earned. Just like all the Gambling Houses and what they take in, it is all planned for the House to Win. Take a good look at this world around YU, there is no mistake here as to the 'Choices and Agreements' that have been made and where everything eventually ends up and who Kontrols all of it. What I am Reporting IS The News, and not about what anyone has, it is all about YU deciding if YU want to Become MoreAware and Recognize Your-Self as a Free Being of Light, or just keep 'Thinking' YU are nothing more than a Human Body and that YU Must Obey with what others have created as nothing more than Restrictions. Have Fun Deciding!

VATICAN VULTURES ARE VICIOUS CRIMINALS & SPIES

Before the known Human History as we know it today, which is mainly 'slanted' from the Kontrolling Kalaum God Korporations, there was an unknown history that has been hidden from this world. As we go back into the Dreary Dark Past of the earth and those who first Kontrolled everyone and everything, we find the Evil Pope. He was the first in charge when the Reptilians Aliens came to the earth and created the human-like humanoids as slaves. This is a part of Human History that is locked away in the vaults of the Ratican at Vatican City in Rome, that very few people know about. The brainwashed audiences only see the smiling and so-called Benevolent Pope, but most people do not know about the Black and Grey Pope who are mainly hidden from the public. More and more people are Waking Up to what has taken place for thousands of years, which has brought this world into its present situation of Corrupt Politics, DarkSide Religion, Militarized Education and Brainwashed Socializm. All of this and so much more has been 'purposely' created to keep people Dumbed Down and Kontrolled. There is no mistake as to what the Invented Governments and their Karmic Religious Kontrolling Gods are doing to everyone.

Look at the Sun in the Sky, do YU see any Kontrol? This IS how Life Really IS! There IS No Kontrol with The Whole of Life! LifeIS not about harassment, intimidation, commandments, rules. regulations, confessions, guidelines, initiations, masters, gurus, disease, infection, virus's, authorities, officialness and so much more silly nonsense that has been planned and implemented to Karmicly Kontrol and steal everything each person has worked for, so that the Presidents, Emperors, Queens, Kings, TapLining Masters, and all the other 'Ruling Factions' can be supported with their Karmic Kontrolling Korporations. The WorldWide WakeUp Call with Duane The Great Writer is for The RealPurpose of Becoming MoreAware Now for Everyone. Everything Duane IS Sharing can be confirmed when YU do The NU-U Sessions and contact Rebazar Tarzs & The RealGuides in Your DreamVisions. There is so much more to a RealLife than this one-dimensional arena, and I suggest YU Start Exploring Now, because it is Your Life Here!!!

EEECKONKON... FLEECING THE MEMBERSHRIMPS FOR GOD

It was 12 Midnight, August 3, 2001. I was standing on The RealSide as I saw Rebazar & Paul talking with HarOld. Rebazar was slowly pacing back and forth in front of HarOld, as Paul stood very still and watched as he smiled. I was a bit curious with the scene and had no concern at all. As Rebazar moved about he would glance at HarOld, and HarOld would then open his eyes a bit wider each time he did.

Then, Rebazar stopped and said very directly to him, "We have given you far too much time with your Joanny Reptilian wife, HarOld. I have warned you many times over the years to keep an eye on her as to what she is always doing to the membership behind their backs with all the TapLining she has been doing. We actually wanted to get rid of you years ago, but Duane was not quite ready yet, and now he is and you are out!!" As HarOld stood and looked at him very surprised.

"But Rebazar, look at all I have done. I have more members and I built the temple for God. I have done very well," he said slowly.

"How many times have I told you before, we do not care about the temple! You listened to Joanny to move everything to Minnesota, so she could hideout and have her way with you. We have given you more than enough time and room to change and you have not. It has become all about the money and control with you and her, as you are both subdued by The Influence from the Kalaum God. You can have your 'religion' and we will have nothing more to do with you. So, now you have the choice to announce Duane, or stay in the Lower Astral Worlds with Your Joanny," said Rebazar, as he and Paul stood back.

HarOld stood for a moment as I watched him trying to decide what to do. I could tell that he really did not want to do this. He looked around and then back at Rebazar and Paul, then he slowly turned and came over to me. As he approached, I could see that his big ears were flat against his head. I could tell that HarOld was not really agreeable with what Rebazar had suggested, but he did 'act' the part.

As he came up to me he said, “He gave me a real taking to. I want to congratulate you, Duane,” he said, as he shook my hand, and then turned and walked over to his TapLined Joanny with The Influence all dressed in black holding her up, as she was unconscious in her arms.

I watched all of them walk off into a misty fog and they were gone, as Rebazar & Paul motioned to me, then gave me The Rod of Power.

HarOld's intent was never to stand aside, because when he did tell the physical Joanny what took place on The RealSide after he returned to his body, she was not at all interested and let him know right away...

“HarOld, you are not going to turn over all that I have worked for to some surfer dude no matter what your stupid masters want!! You are the master and they are all dead!! You put too much faith into this 'dream thing' of yours. I want you to start telling the membership at the seminars that the inner is not important, only being a member and having the initiations matters. For the most part, people are stupid and they want someone to look to. You have been the master for twenty years now and they do not want to see someone new, and if they did a lot of them would leave the membership. Besides, what would we do without my kingdom?” She said, staring at him strongly.

HarOld decided to keep what had been given to him in trust, and now SHE firmly had it all, and with the unconscious MemberShrimps. The rest is Human History and can be read in this NUBook... Have Fun!

~

Reptilian Joanny was sent by the same God of Man that works with the Authoritarians of the Earthly Korporations. Most people look to religion as something that has been defined as 'Holy' when in fact it is far from it. The Planet Earth is Kontrolled from its headquarters in Ratican City, Rome. The Black Pope and his Puppets, such as the Cardinals and the Presidendah of The United States, along with Congress, monitors all the Banking Systems like the Federal Reserve and has created all the World Wars and Cold Wars for the primary purpose of TakeOvers, as The Black Pope uses the US to steal from others for the DarkBrats who rule the planet, then setup their phoney Democratic Government, along with their own hand-picked henchmen as the Political Rulers. It is all Grand Theft on an international scale, and most people have no idea what is really going on. With the internet, many people are Waking Up to Real Human History Now.

And so it has been the same with Reptilian Joanny, as she is tied to the Kalaum God and the Original Reptilian Aliens that first set foot on the Planet Earth and created the humans as slaves to do their tasks. When the first humans were created, they attracted souls from the Astral Worlds who were very low in their consciousness, because the first body types were rather crude, and so they were not given a memory to remember when they reentered each new life. And as time went on, the humanoids became more obedient, because they had gained a lot of experience over lifetimes from the original Reptilian Aliens, as to what to do for their masters. But at some point the humans also began to show more awareness with what they were doing, and so started the rebellions, and so religion was created to psychologically hold people to a more strict routine according to what has become the Priest Craft of today with all the rules and regulations and judgments, and especially with all the intimidation and fear.

With what Paul Twitchell created with Rebazar Tarzs and The Real UNUversal Guides, then with Darwin Gross, and finally HarOld with His Joanny, what was once a unique Way to Reality, has become the Kancerous Karmicly Kontrolled Krone Korporation, with most of the MemberShrimps praying and worshiping the Reptilian God, Kalaum. All the MemberShrimps are TapLined in their dreams with suction lines to their other four Unseen Bodies and Kontrolled by the Alien Influence that rules the Planet Earth. Very few can See this, as it has been so well marketed to be a 'normal standard' for people to eat GMO TechFood, breath poisonous ChemTrail Air, swim in Fukushima Radiated Oceans, drink Fluoridated Water, take lethal Pharmaceutical Drugs, along with Chemo Therapy and Vaccines and be brainwashed with microwaves. Did I leave anything out? I suggest YU read this NUBook and test The NU-U Sessions and Watch Your DreamVisions.

REPTILIAN TAKEOVERS IN HUMAN HISTORY

Because of all the Marketing Ploy and Purposely Planned Deception that has been created throughout the known Human History, the present day population of this world is so Dumbed Down with slanted and perverted nonsense and misinformation, that when Something Wonderful & Real comes along most people resist it. The Reptilian Invented Productions of FearBased FrogHeads (RIPOFF) that of Religion, Education, Politics, Social & SciFi Institutions (REPSystems) mainly rule the earth, which most people are so asleep to that they do not notice what is going on all around them. This does sound like Science Fiction, and it is, as everything in Life is very real as we are experiencing it. We are Now in the Very Scary TechAge, where everyone is a Spy, which does sound funny, but is very real. The DarkBrats who rule the earth, mainly from Ratican City in Rome to the President and Congress of The United States, have Kontrolled this world for thousands of years, and from the beginning of 'their slanted history' when humans were first created as slaves by Reptilians.

The Human History we have today is mainly fabricated, that of the Holy Bible and so many other scriptures that have been created to Kontrol Everyone into a Stupid State (SS) of obedience. It has all been a gradual change over the centuries to where were are Now. Since the day The US Constitution was written and enacted, which was by the DrakBrat Masons, such as George Washington, who designed Washington DC, to Walt Disney, who himself was a Mason and hired by the DarkBrats to create entertainment, as all his movies contain 'subliminal messages' to program people into a Stupid State. There are Reptilians throughout the Religious and Political Systems, along with the Movie Industry, who TapLine and Kontrol people on this physical level, and also in their dreams with their emotional Astral Body. There is so much going on here, but most people are too preoccupied with all the 'flash and phenomena' that has been purposely created to deceive and mislead people into states of stress and confusion to where the planet is totally poisoned and polluted and many people are on drugs, brainwashed by TV and Stupid Political and Religious Speeches, and love to text and put harmful microwave cell phones to their head. Everyone has the right to do whatever they want, but none of this has anything to do with Becoming MoreAware.

Duane The Great Writer is here to provide 'An Adventure Like No Other!' This IS Real Now. DUANEIS THE NUMAN with Rebazar Tarzs & The Real UNUversal Guides, and all other titles and 'master and guru' ideas from 'spiritual paths' along with the Gods of Man, are all outdated and no longer have any substance or substantial value with The TruReality LifeIS, THE ALLIS. The masses have been led to 'believe' Creation is all there is, which is not RealTruth at all, but only 'invented personal truth' Everything Duane is writing can be proven in Your DreamVisions when YU do The NU-U Sessions. All old words such as OM, AUM, HU and others do not have The RealConnection to The SoundLight Reality of THE ALLIS & The RealGuides. The NU-U IS The NUSound and makes a TruConnection to The Whole of Life.

LifeIS AlwaysNU and never old and outdated like all the 'traditional stuff' people carry with their memories, 'thinking' that old stuff is better than Being Now & Real in The RealLight LifeIS. Duane is not a so-called spiritual master, HE IS REAL NOW! Most people will continue to chase their FearBased Religion of the Gods of Man, which has been created to Kontrol people from an emotional level to where they can be TapLined and all their energy taken, along with their money. It is showing up all over today. A good example of this is the Karmicly Kontrolling Krone Korporation (KKKK) ruled by Joanny Klump, adoring wife of TapLining Master HarOld Klump. Joanny was sent by the Kalaum God, Lord God of all Authoritarian Kontrolling Political and Religious Systems of earth and on most of the known RoundWorlds in time and space. All of this and so much more does sound funny, but once YU understand what is really going on with this 'Place in Life' of a planet YU are on, YU will See so much more than just the 'invented silliness' YU have agreed to for the longest time. It is your life, and if YU 'think' this place in space is a good place to live, then YU, like so many others will have the surprise of your life, as all deception shows up. ALLife IS about Becoming MoreAware! What are YU doing Now?

THE KRONIES SPY ON EVERYONE

There are Spies Everywhere! In the USA we have the NSA, the US Government, the Military, Google, Yahoo, Facebook, Dr. Phil and also the Reptilian Owned Krone Korporation, and thousands of others who seem to be so interested in the silliness people do everyday, as we have all been branded as spies and terrorists from the 911 Attack the US Government purposely did on everyone to create more laws to restrict the already restricted public. Joanny and her Puppet TapLine Master HarOld, like to spy on their own MemberShrimps and also me, to make sure they are doing what they are told, like little children who do not know what they are doing. This is what all the governments of the world have been doing for centuries, and with the technology of today, it is a lot easier for them to be everywhere and see everything we are doing, and always according to 'THEM.' This is the earth and this is how it will always be as it will only get worse, even though the Rulers of this planet keep marketing people into the idea they will become more secure with technology. The biggest challenge for most people is to WakeUp and Become MoreAware, because there are so many ways to learn here, but most of the education and old teachings do not get a person out of Creation, which is the PsycRealm Prison.

The DarkBrats who rule the earth have made it a 'standard' to spy on everyone. They want to steal what everyone else has worked for, just like Reptilian Alien Joanny and her TapLine Master HarOld, and they are so afraid they will not have all the control they want over others to do so. They use Marketing Ploy and Project Fear to the masses as they in turn are afraid for themselves of loosing their stupid illusionary power over others, which is nothing more than Agreement. Are these educated people bored or what? Yes they are, because The Whole of LifeIS is not about what YU can get here, IT IS ALL about Your Real Awareniss and not about what can be had on the earth, which will pass away. YU always have the choice to BE Real or stay asleep with the Dumbed Down Humans. The Spies of The Earth will always be around doing their Silly Stuff, as the earth is a 'Place in life' and not Life ITSelf. This can be your time to get out and BE Free... Duane

THE EARTH IS RULED BY ALIEN ASTRAL DECEPTORS

Today, the Political, Religious and Spiritual Systems are nothing more than an invention from the DarkBrats, who rule the earth and other RoundWorlds in time and space for absolute control over the hearts and minds of the unaware masses. There are those who are sincere with their quest to find The TruReality LifeIS, THE ALLIS, and it has come the time where they do not need a Deceptive TapLine Master and to be a follower like a blind cow. The TapLines the Deceptive Masters and their Influential Mates put into people's Astral Bodies is very real. These TapLines drain the person's energy and make them ill and diseased and even to the point of the death of the body. As an example of what is taking place right now, this is what the Krone Korporation does to its paying membershrimps. She, Krone controls the TapLine Master of the Krone Korp. Krone, who is The Influence for millions of Dumbed Down Humans, is a Reptilian TapLiner. She is from the bowels of the lowest Astral Consciousness and wants to have the earth for herself. When the time comes, she will eat her Old Master like a Black Widow. This is the earth today and She loves it.

THE NUMAN with Rebazar Tarzs & The Real UNUversal Guides are here to Share Their RealExperiences for Everyone to Recognize and to Become MoreAware and to BE Free from the Causes and Effects of Creation. The TapLine Masters will always control the earth and the unaware and there will be very few who have the courage to Become Real RiskTakers and Recognize THE ALLIS. The Deceptive Systems of today are merely Old Traditional Nonsense and have nothing to do with The Real & Wonderful UNUverses of THE ALLIS. When YU do The NU-U Sessions and Watch Your DreamVisions, YU will be shown by Rebazar Tarzs & The RealGuides what is taking place with the Earthly Korporations and their Deceptive TapLine Masters. With The Natural Environment that supports ALL of US there are no masters or memberships. The Sun in the sky is AlwaysNU & Real, and it is a very good reference for ALL of US to better understand where we are while we are in a human body. Life makes sense, and when YU can See Beyond the Marketing Ploy of the TapLine Masters, YU are Free!

TAPLINE MASTERS ARE EVERYWHERE

The average person has no idea they have four other bodies they carry besides the solid physical vehicle. Just because the Invented Systems of Scientific Experimentation cannot prove the existence of all the unseen bodies of man does not mean they do not exist. It takes a very special person to be able to See the Astral, Causal, Mental and Etheric Bodies, and also The RealAwareniss, RealU. On earth, people are living a one-dimensional life and not much more. Everyone is always relating to other levels and dimensions, but for the most part, they do not See or understand this nor themselves and what they are capable of. What is really going on would shock the hell out of people if they could See it, and that is the TapLines they have in them from all the 'Agreements' they have made over lifetimes with those who control them. In a way, it is like the 'Bonding' idea of today, which may sound cute, but can lead to medical situations that a person definitely would not do to themselves if they knew what is being deliberately placed in their inner bodies as an absolute control.

TapLines are Very Real, and they do effect the physical body, even though they are placed in one of the four unseen bodies. Today, we have Kalaum God Korporate Masters, such as there are with spiritual paths, Industrial Korporations and Business Korps. There is always someone at the head of these Korporations, like a master or CEO, and they want to make sure that those who take part in what these Korps are marketing 'Agree' and are TapLined, especially from their Astral, Emotional Body. From the 'Front' they have created with their Marketing Ploy, it would seem that what the KorpMasters are doing 'looks' really good, but when YU See what is taking place from The RealSide in Your DreamVisions, YU will See all the TapLines a person has from the deception of the Outer Business Fronts. The days of Masters and Gurus are gone! This IS Real Now! YU are a Free Being of Light and YU do not need to 'follow or worship' anything or anyone unless YU want to. ALLife IS Free and never restricted like the KorpMasters have created their 'Business Plans of Deception' with their 'Membership' ideas of Absolute Control. The Old Traditional

Ways are nothing more than Planned Deception to TapLine people into an unconscious submission of control to support whatever system or business they have created. The 'spiritual' idea has been used by politics and religion for thousands of years, and it those who own these Deceptive Systems that get people to Agree to a TapLined LifeStyle of Obedience. Worshiping anything is stupid, unless it is The TruReality LifeIS, THE ALLIS. With THE ALLIS, there is no worship or sacrifices or Support Systems, there is only Being Real & Wonderful & Becoming MoreAware. ALL of US are Radiant Beings of RealLight!

Most people do not understand where they are as they are living on this planet. They 'think' in terms as they have by being herded to 'think' like cattle, that the earth is the only 'Place in Life' where there is any life, and that the Gods of Man shine upon those who 'believe' in them. All of this and so much more is a Deceptive Marketing Ploy that has been cleverly devised to control the emotions and mind of each person to get them to work for those who do not want to do their share as equals, but as self-appointed Kings, Queens, Presidents, Masters, Rulers, Dictators, Emperors, Royalty, Know-It-Alls, and so many other 'titles' that entice people to bow and kneel and 'think' that someone is special because they can make more money than others and own more on the earth, as an example. What a person has with their life is their right, but it does not create a difference of any kind, only people do with their 'little thinking' and by Agreeing to Being Limited by what others create. Because people are Marketed to Agree, they many times become TapLined, just like when YU are on your computer and YU surf the Internet, YU pickup 'cookies' and other things from the 'browsing' YU do. The same is Very Real with Agreeing to the Deceptive Systems of the earth, they TapLine YU and even control YU in Your DreamVisions. If YU do The NU-U Sessions and have The RealConnection with The SoundLight Reality of THE ALLIS, Rebazar Tarzs & The Real UNUversal Guides of THE IS, will protect YU from the Mischievous TapLines of Old KorpMasters and The Influence that rules and weaves its ways in the PsycRealms. YU always have the 'Choice' and really do not need anything, simply BE Wonderful with The RealGuidance and RealEducation of Becoming MoreAware Now!

ROMANTIC ADVENTURES LIKE NO OTHER
AND ALL FOR JUST YOU!

Virtually, all of us have read stories and seen movies that are far beyond our imagination, and we love them! We want to be a part of them, we want to be the characters in the story or the star of the movie. Most people have been taught that they can only dream such things, and this is true, but The Reality of ALL Realities IS, that we can each have a life better than we can ever imagine if we are willing to have RealGuidance and a RealEducation to have such a life. It takes a person that is willing to have the courage to be a Real RiskTaker, a non conformist in such a special way, a person that is not rebellious, but daring and resourceful, creative and ingenious. I am not referring to one who is over educated and intellectual, but moreso street smart from the experiences they have from the world around them. If then, they are willing to climb a mountain higher than they ever have and See what very few ever will, they may be ready to gain the first steps of True Insight beyond what their personal mind will ever know, and it is all so Real, so much so, that even what they can imagine will never equal what they will experience with The TruReality of Themselves.

Most of the masses have been taught to look to something outside of themselves, such as their parents, teachers, saviors, saints, and even the gods people have decided upon to worship as their authorities, but The Real Challenge and Real Adventure is already with each of us, but we must have RealGuidance and a Real Education to be able to first Recognize it. The socialized public is educated into a one-dimensional Literal Sense, and basically nothing is taught about a person's insight, intuition, and most importantly, their perception beyond what they can even imagine that can be possible. The Whole of Life, The TruReality Life Already IS, cannot be contained in any descriptive form, such as an idea that applies to our physical life. It can be so that a person can think and decide whatever they want to, but when a person has Real Experiences beyond what their mind and imagination has never experienced, then they will be able to enter unseen dimensions and realities that cannot be defined with words and ideas, but can only become alive by the person who is having the experience. A person can read books about being a pilot, but if they never fly an airplane, then they never have The Real Experience of doing it. Each one of us is so much more than just a physical body and mind. We each actually have four other bodies, and what oversees these bodies is our RealAwareness. But, to get to The RealU, one must have RealGuidance, because there is so much to each of us that is not seen on the surface and lies hidden, even to ourselves. To discover ourselves we must become The RiskTaker.

The masses, those flock of people who have in some way agreed to be educated and herded into categories that others have invented as a control over the unaware, will almost always follow their Literal Senses, their educated upbringing, which seems to fit so nicely into the social stream of things. But, The Real RiskTaker does not follow the herd, and is exceptional in their thinking, creativity, and they have taken the time to developed their insight, intuition, and most of all, The TruPerception Life IS. Those who try and walk The Razors Edge, usually fall short of The TruReality Life IS, because what I am referring to here is so much more than the Gods of Man, and all the authorities of the earth with their supposed educated wisdom. The TruReality Life IS, is So Real, Pure and Genuine, that it is definitely so that one cannot imagine that such a Reality even exists, IT IS That Real!

It is not up to me to convince anyone about what I am presenting here, but for sure, anyone can easily prove with themselves that they truly are so much more than a body on earth and what they are thinking with their mind. Peter Pan, did not want to go with Wendy, because he knew he would be educated and grow old. Until one is willing to come to grips with themselves and decide to explore what most people never will, then they will merely grow old and never have the life they really wanted that lies beyond their dreams. The TruReality Life IS, is so much greater than any fantasy one can imagine, it is The Amazing Romantic Adventure everyone is looking for from all the Invented Systems, but will never be found here. Only those who have The Heart for a Real Life will know, 'What IS Real.'

HUMANS ARE PURPOSELY DUMBED DOWN

The Business World of today is based upon a lot of deception and seems to be okay with most people. Duane The Great Writer is merely 'Reporting the News,' and what each person does with this information is their free will. If people do not mind looking silly and actually stupid to those who control Big Business, then they are the people that can enjoy staying asleep to what is really taking place on the planet earth within the created social structures. But, as a hint, there is a much bigger picture that is possible for everyone, even bigger than knowing what is really taking place with the Deceptions of Big Business. This report must have a beginning, and so it will start off with the world around us and what all of us have participated in and have created for ourselves. The Big Businesses that create the most deception to everyone are the government agencies, and mostly those at the head of the government. It must be so that these highly educated intellects and Literalists, always happen to forget to tell the onlooking public that they are really a corporation all their own and not part of what has been looked to as the US Government. But, in some strange way they have got total control over the monetary system and all those who accept their pretty speeches with whatever they say and imply. They make the rules and make them sound really good, as though what they are doing will actually help those they supposedly serve, but again, there is a bigger picture here. With the Internet, it is easy to research what has and is taking place with those in control.

The funny thing is, most people really do not want to look behind the curtain, as the Dumbed Down Humans have been taught more about what they should 'fear' than that of a broader and better understanding of themselves and the world around them. The political speeches of politicians, and this can include religious and educational deceptors who are in bed with Big Business, are usually a lot of hot air to the public, and if there is a benefit somewhere, it is usually always for those making the hot air speeches. What is being presented here is not whether a person 'believes' this or not, but it must be up to each to investigate for themselves if there is any truth to what is being told by the Big Business Politicians. The US Government, which is supposed to be related in some realistic way to The Bill of Rights and The US Constitution, as an example, is the Biggest Business there is. Maybe when the Cowboys and Indians were running around, the declarations originally created for all citizens had some kind of meaning, but over the years, just about all of what was proposed has become put in the shadows, and now we have things like the Patriot Act, which is a perfect deception for those who created it. And another example, the so-called 'deficit' that always seems to be an issue with the US Government and is constantly projected onto the American public. Has all been another planned deception to hold people to fear.

People are always asking the basic question... Why does the US Government do this or that? Well, it is all very simple once a person has the right information and knowledge and can See Beyond what is told to them from the mouth-pieces known as the elected officials. But, it people want to stay asleep, thinking in their little radiated and controlled minds they are safer to be ignorant of what is always being taken advantage of them, they have that right. For those who want to know, then it is suggested to start with the Federal Reserve Act of 1913, as one example. I am really going in baby steps here, because the more a person knows the more it begins to appear to be science fiction to them. The 'deficit' that has been created has been purposely done so for a very simple reason, to bind people, then to eventually take every-thing they have worked for. There is so much more to this, as there are no mistakes with the US Government, and they know perfectly well what they have been doing all along. By investigating what Big Business has done to create their monetary system, first of all for themselves, then institute all kinds of government agencies as their backup, and making it look as though they are creating new jobs and helping people, is all a planned deception to make the public prisoners. Of course, there is the beneficial side, as there are to all things. When Hitler imprisoned the Jews, he still housed and fed them, so there is still an advantage to what the US Government is doing and will do in the future, like putting as many people as possible into the already available FEMA Camps across America.

Those who rule the earth have a great fear themselves, and that is with all the billions of people on the planet that could become aware of what they are really doing, thus rebelling and they themselves taking control. So, the Elite, the few who do control the money system and hundreds of millions of government workers, from the lifeguards on the beach, the park rangers, the red cross, the police, the FBI, the CIA, National Security, the UN, the Council on Foreign Affairs, and whatever government agency that has been created for the so-called betterment of mankind, has all been strategically placed to protect those that imprison all the Dumbed Down Humans. The reason most people will not take the time to investigate what is really taking place on their own planet is because they are too afraid to. The idea of 'fear' has been driven into everyone for thousands of lifetimes and everyone carries their own unconscious fear with them, whether they agree to it or not. Until each person decides to confront their own illusions about what they have so easily accepted and agreed to, then they will stay asleep for lifetimes to come with the Elites as their masters and controllers. As a person sleeps with their embodiment, they are the effect of everything around them, and most of all themselves.

As one gets into the heart of what is really taking place on the earth, far aside from their daily routine of having a good job, living in a nice house, raising the family and going to Disneyland once in a while, they will discover that the Passing dream they are in is not at all what they have been taught it was or supposed to be. There is a total-takeover going on and all Dumbed Down Humans are the effect of this, and the end result will show up as something appearing like 'The Lord of The Rings.' Human history, the real side of it that is, reveals what has already taking place and is an excellent indicator of what everything is now moving into now. But of course, the Dumbed Down Humans of the past never listened then, as in the case of seeing Noah building his ark and trying to warn people. There is no part of real human experience that is religious, as religion is part of the Big Business role model for people to relate to as a means of control. The One World Order Brats, have so many different diversities for people to get lost in, so that they can secretly go about their business of a complete and total takeover of all material things, and even the thoughts and ideas people create. Again, they do not want any competition, as they fear being second best and taken over themselves.

With what is being presented here is not a matter that a person become involved with some sort of petitions or demonstrations, nor a rebellion of any kind, not at all! Nor pray for relief from the gods mankind has worshiped, which the Elites have actually invented to subdue the masses into another type of dream world that never resolves itself. It is true there are heavens above the earth, and there are gods, Angels and saviors, but again, there is a much bigger picture that is not seen or has been experienced by most, and this is what this NUBook is all about. But then again, very few people will have the courage to test and explore what is within this writing. It is really all about the programing all of us have gone through for untold lifetimes. Once this is understood and where all created things have really come from, then one can begin their own Real Journey into Life. There is almost unlimited information and knowledge on the earth, and especially with the Internet, so in today's world, everyone has a much greater advantage than ever before to free themselves from the tyranny that will always reign the earth. The idea here is to Become MoreAware, and by doing so, and with RealGuidance, a person can learn to become aware of their RealAwareness, beyond that of the five embodiments they are operating and have succumb to.

All of us the ability to create, and because each of us have free will, we can do whatever we want to. This then becomes the fine line as to what each person will choose to do with their life and what they will create. This presentation is not about what a person should do with their life and their creative abilities, but moreso about Becoming More Aware. The Reality of Becoming MoreAware, does start of with the elementary stages all of us go through as we grow and mature with our physical body, mind and emotions, but there is so much more than is not seen on the surface, or even thought of, and eventually cannot even be imagined. So, all of us must start from somewhere to better understand where we are with The Whole of Life, moreso than just what our personal physical life entails. The average person will be raised by their parents and then become educated according to the society they were raised in. From there, they will decide a role for themselves to survive by. Survival is the key factor. Not how smart one is, or highly educated they are, but moreso how one can adapt and survive the environment they are in. The Real Meaning of Becoming MoreAware is not about any ancient wisdom or spiritual quest the people of this world have experienced. The Real Meaning of Becoming MoreAware goes beyond all that a person has come to know from the different sources of education on earth. There are many stages to Becoming MoreAware of survival. All of us are experiencing what we have become used to as our survival while we have a physical body here, but there is so much more. The next stage would be something along the lines of what takes place after the body ceases and a person crosses over to the next level in Life. Everyone will have their own experience of what is termed as 'death,' according to how they have been taught and have accepted and agreed to what they have been educated with while they were on earth. From a human view, it would seem that what one learns here is the ultimate in some ways, but this place is actually the bottom of Life.

So, from here it can only get better and the same with with survival. On the earth, survival is a struggling daily occurrence, whereas, as one ascends into higher levels of Life, survival gets easier and a lot better and more assured. So why is it that so many people are so afraid to leave this place? Simply because, they have been taught to fear The Whole of Life, instead of better understanding it. Here again is where Big Business has stepped in and purposely manipulated and distorted people's educational process into tiny miniscule views of aberrations and purposely driven fears. Why? All for control! The interesting thing is, those who fear the most, such as the DarkBrats who rule the earth, will always be out to get others, so others will fear them, and so they will have control over them. This is all absurd of course, but it is the mainframe of Big Business right now. For those who do not want to see what is taking place and pretend that it does not exist, then their survival level will be according to how they can handle the reality of what is really taking place on this planet when it hits them. Life makes sense, and each person has the opportunity to make sense of it for themselves by exploring The Reality of What Life IS, or they can stay asleep and see what happens. The Reality Life IS, cannot be found in any educational institution, be it social, political or religious. The reason the planet is overly polluted and diseased is not because of anything The Natural Environment, or the creatures and animals have contributed, it is all from what humans have decided with how they have become overly creative. Yet, most people keep asking why is this all happening, and also praying for things to change and get better, when in fact most people want to stay the same with all the polluting they are doing. Everyone does have a choice to better survive, but the majority keep agreeing to those who are actually the ones involved with destroying The Natural Environment.

All of this is very simple again, Big Business and Big Profits! People's lives do not matter, because the Elites can clone more bodies, as they have technology far past what the public has ever heard of. This again has nothing to do with a person 'believing' this or that, because it is all happening right in front of us all. The weather is manipulated with ChemTrails, which are toxic poisons to everything on the planet. The food production is mainly Genetically Modified (GMO) for now, but will soon be nothing but. Big Pharma, owns the life span of so many people, and there are more getting lethal drugings everyday, as it is Big Business as usual. The drinking water has been laced with Sodium Fluoride, which the public was told helps a person's teeth, when in fact there is no such creature on the elemental scale as Sodium Fluoride, which in fact causes all kinds of health issues. Hitler and Stalin used Sodium Fluoride to Dumb Down The Humans. Then, there is the lethal vaccines that have been marketed to provide a remedy, but are actually very toxic and have caused many deaths and put a lot of children and adults in comas and caused paralysis. Again, who is it that is behind all this? The US Government! The politicians are the paid puppets of the One World Order DarkBrats. Politicians run the show for the audience, while the Elite Bankers from behind the scenes create their Computer Money to fund all the wars and agitation that has been experienced by many and is being seen today.

The Big Business World Takeovers, pivot off the Federal Reserve Act of 1913, as one of the major examples of what life on earth is today. Understanding the Monetary System, especially if a person wants to live in a social structure created by others, should be an educational adventure to explore. Being involved in some way with the earth is why we are here, but each of us makes the choice as to how we want to participate. What a person decides is not so much about good or bad, but moreso about Cause and Effect. What all of us have created has become what we now have to deal with, and there are many ways to do this. Some people have decided to petition and demonstrate once they understand what is taking place, and the Elites are always ready for this, as they have passed laws totally shadowing The Bill of Rights and The US Constitution, for the very purpose of containing and controlling the masses. The DarkBrats are always ahead of the mob thinkers. As in the case of World War I & II, as they were both purposely planned in the late 1800's, as Big Business Ventures and as takeovers. Of course, where in the history books is this explained? It never will be, because the public wants to hear something nice like pretty speeches, so the politicians make sure that all the educational systems have socially indoctrinated material to where each and every person can be personally and subliminally manipulated.

This introduction is such a miniscule portion of what is really taking place with all the Big Business Deception on the planet today. So, it is up to each person to learn to fend for themselves when it comes to surviving while they are here. There is always RealGuidance that is available Now, but most people will cling to what they have always known, and especially to the Invented Political and Religious Systems who rule the earth. Who is it that really rules the earth? For those who are interested, the knowledge is always available, but how many have the real courage to identify it and then do Something Real, like Becoming MoreAware? As one reads this NUBook, they will be taken into NUWorlds and Universes, the likes of which most know nothing about. It is not scary at all...It is ALL Wonderful! Have Fun Deciding!

DUMBED DOWN HUMANS

With all the modern conveniences we have, it would seem that we are in just the right spot with Human History as it IS Now, but far from it! Most people have been so Dumbed Down for untold centuries, and they actually carry a huge amount of misinformation with them all the time from their pastlives. All of us do have our own experiences and our own 'truths and realities,' but what we are experiencing on this Matrixed Hologram known as earth, is merely a 'Place in Life' and nothing more. For those who have consciously left their bodies, and especially at night when the physical embodiment sleeps, they know what is being referred to here. Everyone is having Out of Body Experiences, and many are not recognizing this fact or they do not remember their dreams. And, there are those who will not admit it to themselves, and especially to others about their Out of Body Experiences, whatever! Duane The Great Writer, is on earth at this time to provide a RealService, one of informing the public that they can now escape from the earth and all the Authoritarians who rule here, that is if they have The Real Courage to do so. A person must firmly decide they want to See Beyond what is always outside of them, this world of fabricated 'fronts.' Duane, is not here to change anything, he is simply here to provide a NUAvenue to The TruReality Life IS, beyond the Invented Systems and those who rule the earth and even the heavens people look to. Watch Your DreamVisions at night!

Dumbed Down Humans have been taught to 'believe' in something, but The Whole of Life is so much bigger and better than any 'belief' can contain. So, a person must become a Real RiskTaker, or they will never experience The TruReality Life IS. It truly takes a lot of Real Guidance and Real Education for one to even start to understand a small portion of what Duane is presenting with his NUBooks in 'The AdventurIS Series.' The Dumbed Down Humans of the earth, have been purposely put to sleep about all that is really taking place on this planet and what is right in front of them all the time. There is no mistake as to all the pollution and destruction this world is experiencing everyday, as most of it is very well planned as part of the overall takeover for the entire human race. Yes, this does sound like science fiction, but so would a cell be so to the Cowboys and Indians in their day. It is time for people to 'Wakeup' or be totally taken over by the Invented Systems and their diabolical plans to have everyone here as their slaves as they are now and into future lifetimes. Of course, like Noah telling the villages about the great flood coming, which was not about any doom, but simply a warning, Duane is doing the same thing, and each person can prove what is written here to themselves. If you as the reader will simply 'test' what is being presented here, then you will soon Become MoreAware and conscious in Your DreamVisions of The RealGuidance that can be with you always, then See for yourself from The RealSide of Life what has and is taking place on earth Now. There is no mystery about anything in Life. The only mysteries there are is the lack of knowledge and experience a person has and is willing to go for, so Take The Risk and Have Fun!

Out of Body Experiences have been recorded for thousands of years. These extraordinary events are throughout many historical writings, art and music, and even the Bible. Even Jesus was referring to Out of Body Experiences when he spoke of the 'Many Mansions,' that could be visited while one was still on earth. He was referring to the many heavens and levels that already exist with Life. As an example, when parts of the Bible are taken 'literally,' a clear picture of what is being presented is not Seen. It should also be noted that The Whole of Life has nothing to do with religion, politics, or any of the educational systems that have been created here. All these things are man made and that's as far as they go. Once a person has Real Guidance with Rebazar Tarzs and The Real Universal Guides, they will be shown from a much higher view what is really taking place on the earth today. Duane, has provided The NU-U Session, for people to start their own Journey to Real Freedom. By testing The NU-U Sessions, a person can learn to contact The SoundLight Reality Life IS, and The RealGuidance will be with them as they release themselves from their confined physical shell and explore beyond this realm into The Real Universes. Because humans have been taught a one-dimensional reality and lifestyle, they do not have the proper knowledge about Out of Body Experiences. A person can read about someone having such experiences, but when it comes to their own life they are in the dark, so to speak. OBE, is a very simple and subtle occurrence that everyone is doing, but not recognizing the fact they are doing it.

By having conscious OBE, a person can learn to save their own life from their own Cause and Effect Karma, and also having to reincarnate on the earth ever again. The RealGuides teach each person how to rise above this Passing Dream World of limited embodiments and soon enter The Real Universes, far beyond the psychic realms of the Astral, and Mental Worlds. The heavens of Man, are actually very limited, and everyone has already been there many times, but most people do not remember, because they have taken on a new body and mind each time they return here. The Religious and Political Systems of the earth are not interested in the welfare of the individual, their only purpose is to keep as many souls as possible reincarnating into future lifetimes as their Kontrollable Servants once again. Anyone can learn to figure out what is being presented here for themselves, if they will take the time and get past their own fears of suppression from the authorities who rule over them. OBE is not rocket science, but a very simple application of paying attention to one's own awareness and learning to Become MoreAware. There is no rebellion of any kind with any of this, but simply to decide to want to know RealTruth beyond all the 'truths' that one has come to know from being here. You can Take The Risk or stay as you have been.

If you you are one of those who just sits back and says “I don't believe this or that,' every time someone tries to share something with you, then this is probably not for you, because you just want to stay asleep and go with the 'Invasion of The Body Snatchers.' What is being referred to here is very real, but from all the Marketing Ploy that has been established with almost every person on the planet, it now becomes a huge undertaking for anyone to get through their own Designed Consciousness and all they have agreed to. The only doom that has ever taken place on this planet for the most part is from the Dumbed Down Humans themselves. It is already noted that very few people will actually wakeup to all that is taking place on earth today, but Duane is making an effort to let others know what is right in front of them. ALL LIFE IS NOW! This is a realty not taught in any school, because the Invented Political, Religious, Educational and Social Systems, do not want people to think for themselves, but only listen to 'political pretty words and speeches,' that are created to direct people into a somber sleep state where they are submissive to their rulers. All of this has been going on for centuries, and there are some people who have woken up, but there is a lot more to go. Many of those who have awakened to the takeovers in the world today are still not Seeing the entire picture that is possible to view from where they are standing. Duane The Great Writer cannot tell people everything, because there is far too much to each of us in our RealAwareniss. So, for those who simply take the time to read one of The NUBooks, they will definitely learn a lot. If you as the Reader actually any of The NUBooks, your life will never be the same. Test The NU-U Sessions and Take The Risk to SeeMore then before... Have Fun Deciding!

WE ARE PROVIDING A
WORLDWIDE WAKEUP CALL FOR EVERYONE

SEE US ON FACEBOOK AND YOUTUBE:

'DUANE THE GREAT WRITER'

'ALLSOLAR RESEARCH VESSEL'

'ASK EVA NOW' / 'EVA KNOWS'

www.DuaneTheGreatWriter.info

DuaneTheGreatWriter@inbox.com

SEND US AN EMAIL AND DUANE&EVA WILL SEND YU A NUBOOK!

THE ADVENTURIS SERIES

Book One
'FROM THEN TO NOW'

Book Two
'A JOURNEY TO REALFREEDOM'

Book Three
'THE REAL FAR COUNTRY'

Book Four
'THE ADVENTURES OF REBAZAR TARZS'

Book Five
'THE NUWAVIS THE ROD OF POWER'

Book Six
'YOUR DREAMVISIONS'

Book Seven
'THE NUWAVIS SON OF REBAZAR'

Book Eight
'BLUE SKY ISLAND'

THE TRUCOMPLETENESS COURSE FOR REALFREEEDOM NOW

www.ingramcontent.com/pod-product-compliance
Ingram Content Group UK Ltd.
Pitfield, Milton Keynes, MK11 3LW, UK
UKHW041925190726
13854UKWH00003B/1448

9 781312 665118